Civil Democratic Islam

Partners, Resources, and Strategies

Cheryl Benard

Supported by the Smith Richardson Foundation

RAND

National Security Research Division

The research described in this report was sponsored by the Smith Richardson Foundation.

Library of Congress Cataloging-in-Publication Data

Benard, Cheryl, 1953-
 Civil democratic Islam, partners, resources, and strategies / Cheryl Benard.
  p. cm.
 "MR-1716."
 Includes bibliographical references.
 ISBN 0-8330-3438-3 (pbk.)
  1. Islam and civil society. 2. Islamic modernism. 3. Democracy—Religious aspects—Islam. 4. Islam—University. 5. Islam—21st century. I.Title.

BP173.63 .B46 2003
320.5'5'0917671—dc21

2003012442

The RAND Corporation is a nonprofit research organization providing objective analysis and effective solutions that address the challenges facing the public and private sectors around the world. RAND's publications do not necessarily reflect the opinions of its research clients and sponsors.

RAND® is a registered trademark.

Cover design by Eileen Delson La Russo

Published 2003 by the RAND Corporation
1700 Main Street, P.O. Box 2138, Santa Monica, CA 90407-2138
1200 South Hayes Street, Arlington, VA 22202-5050
201 North Craig Street, Suite 202, Pittsburgh, PA 15213-1516
RAND URL: http://www.rand.org/
To order RAND documents or to obtain additional information, contact Distribution Services: Telephone: (310) 451-7002;
Fax: (310) 451-6915; Email: order@rand.org

The Islamic world is involved in a struggle to determine its own nature and values, with serious implications for the future. What role can the rest of the world, threatened and affected as it is by this struggle, play in bringing about a more peaceful and positive outcome?

Devising a judicious approach requires a finely grained understanding of the ongoing ideological struggle within Islam, to identify appropriate partners and set realistic goals and means to encourage its evolution in a positive way.

The United States has three goals in regard to politicized Islam. First, it wants to prevent the spread of extremism and violence. Second, in doing so, it needs to avoid the impression that the United States is "opposed to Islam." And third, in the longer run, it must find ways to help address the deeper economic, social, and political causes feeding Islamic radicalism and to encourage a move toward development and democratization.

The debates and conflicts that mark the current Islamic world can make the picture seem confusing. It becomes easier to sort the actors if one thinks of them not as belonging to distinct categories but as falling along a **spectrum**. Their views on certain critical **marker issues** help to locate them correctly on this spectrum.

It is then possible to see which part of the spectrum is generally compatible with our values, and which is fundamentally inimical. On this basis, this report identifies components of a specific strategy.

This report should be of interest to scholars, policymakers, students, and all others interested in the Middle East, Islam, and political Islam.

CONTENTS

TABLE

There is no question that contemporary Islam is in a volatile state, engaged in an internal and external struggle over its values, its identity, and its place in the world. Rival versions are contending for spiritual and political dominance. This conflict has serious costs and economic, social, political, and security implications for the rest of the world. Consequently, the West is making an increased effort to come to terms with, to understand, and to influence the outcome of this struggle.

Clearly, the United States, the modern industrialized world, and indeed the international community as a whole would prefer an Islamic world that is compatible with the rest of the system: democratic, economically viable, politically stable, socially progressive, and follows the rules and norms of international conduct. They also want to prevent a "clash of civilizations" in all of its possible variants—from increased domestic unrest caused by conflicts between Muslim minorities and "native" populations in the West to increased militancy across the Muslim world and its consequences, instability and terrorism.

It therefore seems judicious to encourage the elements within the Islamic mix that are most compatible with global peace and the international community and that are friendly to democracy and modernity. However, correctly identifying these elements and finding the most suitable way to cooperate with them is not always easy.

Islam's current crisis has two main components: a failure to thrive and a loss of connection to the global mainstream. The Islamic world has been marked by a long period of backwardness and comparative powerlessness; many different solutions, such as nationalism, pan-Arabism, Arab socialism, and Islamic revolution, have been attempted without success, and this has led to frustration and anger. At the same time, the Islamic world has fallen out of step with contemporary global culture, an uncomfortable situation for both sides.

Muslims disagree on what to do about this, and they disagree on what their society ultimately should look like. We can distinguish four essential positions:

- **Fundamentalists** reject democratic values and contemporary Western culture. They want an authoritarian, puritanical state that will implement their extreme view of Islamic law and morality. They are willing to use innovation and modern technology to achieve that goal.

- **Traditionalists** want a conservative society. They are suspicious of modernity, innovation, and change.

- **Modernists** want the Islamic world to become part of global modernity. They want to modernize and reform Islam to bring it into line with the age.

- **Secularists** want the Islamic world to accept a division of church and state in the manner of Western industrial democracies, with religion relegated to the private sphere.

These groups hold distinctly different positions on essential issues that have become contentious in the Islamic world today, including political and individual freedom, education, the status of women, criminal justice, the legitimacy of reform and change, and attitudes toward the West.

The **fundamentalists** are hostile to the West and to the United States in particular and are intent, to varying degrees, on damaging and destroying democratic modernity. Supporting them is not an option, except for transitory tactical considerations. The **traditionalists** generally hold more moderate views, but there are significant differences between different groups of traditionalists. Some are close to the fundamentalists. None wholeheartedly embraces modern democracy and the culture and values of modernity and, at best, can only make an uneasy peace with them.

The **modernists** and **secularists** are closest to the West in terms of values and policies. However, they are generally in a weaker position than the other groups, lacking powerful backing, financial resources, an effective infrastructure, and a public platform. The **secularists**, besides sometimes being unacceptable as allies on the basis of their broader ideological affiliation, also have trouble addressing the traditional sector of an Islamic audience.

Traditional orthodox Islam contains democratic elements that can be used to counter the repressive, authoritarian Islam of the fundamentalists, but it is not suited to be the primary vehicle of democratic Islam. That role falls to the Islamic modernists, whose effectiveness, however, has been limited by a number of constraints, which this report will explore.

To encourage positive change in the Islamic world toward greater democracy, modernity, and compatibility with the contemporary international world order, the United States and the West need to consider very carefully which elements, trends, and forces within Islam they intend to strengthen; what the goals and values of their various potential allies and protégés really are; and what the broader consequences of advancing their respective agendas are likely to be. A mixed approach composed of the following elements is likely to be the most effective:

- **Support the modernists first:**
    - — Publish and distribute their works at subsidized cost.
    - — Encourage them to write for mass audiences and for youth.
    - — Introduce their views into the curriculum of Islamic education.
    - — Give them a public platform.
    - — Make their opinions and judgments on fundamental questions of religious interpretation available to a mass audience in competition with those of the fundamentalists and traditionalists, who have Web sites, publishing houses, schools, institutes, and many other vehicles for disseminating their views.
    - — Position secularism and modernism as a "counterculture" option for disaffected Islamic youth.
    - — Facilitate and encourage an awareness of their pre- and non-Islamic history and culture, in the media and the curricula of relevant countries.
    - — Assist in the development of independent civic organizations, to promote civic culture and provide a space for ordinary citizens to educate themselves about the political process and to articulate their views.
- **Support the traditionalists against the fundamentalists:**
    - — Publicize traditionalist criticism of fundamentalist violence and extremism; encourage disagreements between traditionalists and fundamentalists.
    - — Discourage alliances between traditionalists and fundamentalists.
    - — Encourage cooperation between modernists and the traditionalists who are closer to the modernist end of the spectrum.
    - — Where appropriate, educate the traditionalists to equip them better for debates against fundamentalists. Fundamentalists are often rhetorically superior, while traditionalists practice a politically inarticulate "folk Islam." In such places as Central Asia, they may need to be educated and trained in orthodox Islam to be able to stand their ground.
    - — Increase the presence and profile of modernists in traditionalist institutions.

- — Discriminate between different sectors of traditionalism. Encourage those with a greater affinity to modernism, such as the Hanafi law school, versus others. Encourage them to issue religious opinions and popularize these to weaken the authority of backward Wahhabi-inspired religious rulings. This relates to funding: Wahhabi money goes to the support of the conservative Hanbali school. It also relates to knowledge: More-backward parts of the Muslim world are not aware of advances in the application and interpretation of Islamic law.

- — Encourage the popularity and acceptance of Sufism.

- **Confront and oppose the fundamentalists:**
  - — Challenge their interpretation of Islam and expose inaccuracies.
  - — Reveal their linkages to illegal groups and activities.
  - — Publicize the consequences of their violent acts.
  - — Demonstrate their inability to rule, to achieve positive development of their countries and communities.
  - — Address these messages especially to young people, to pious traditionalist populations, to Muslim minorities in the West, and to women.
  - — Avoid showing respect or admiration for the violent feats of fundamentalist extremists and terrorists. Cast them as disturbed and cowardly, not as evil heroes.
  - — Encourage journalists to investigate issues of corruption, hypocrisy, and immorality in fundamentalist and terrorist circles.
  - — Encourage divisions among fundamentalists.

- **Selectively support secularists:**
  - — Encourage recognition of fundamentalism as a shared enemy, discourage secularist alliance with anti-U.S. forces on such grounds as nationalism and leftist ideology.
  - — Support the idea that religion and the state can be separate in Islam too and that this does not endanger the faith but, in fact, may strengthen it.

Whichever approach or mix of approaches is chosen, we recommend that it be done with careful deliberation, in knowledge of the symbolic weight of certain issues; the meaning likely to be assigned to the alignment of U.S. policymakers with particular positions on these issues; the consequences of these alignments for other Islamic actors, including the risk of endangering or discrediting the very groups and people we are seeking to help; and the opportunity costs and possible unintended consequences of affiliations and postures that may seem appropriate in the short term.

ACKNOWLEDGMENTS

I would like to thank Zalmay Khalilzad, Jerrold Green, Theodore Karasik, Angel Rabasa, Phyllis Gilmore, Luetta Pope, Joanna Alberdeston, and Robin Cole for their comments, suggestions, and assistance with this report.

burqa	The voluminous, all-covering outer garment worn by Afghan women
fatwa	A formal pronouncement on a doctrinal or legal matter by an Islamic scholar or scholarly body
hadith	A narrated story relating to the actions or sayings of the prophet Muhammad and his closest followers, presumed to reflect the correct way of doing things and to supplement the guidance given in the Quran. An exacting science has been created around the need to substantiate and verify hadith, but the very hugeness of the body of hadith makes it subject to accidental or intentional misuse.
Hanafi	One of the schools of Islamic law; more liberal on most matters
Hanbali	One of the schools of Islamic law; more conservative on most matters
hijab	Literally, the Islamic "dress code" for women; the term can be used to refer to the simple headscarf or to more elaborate coverings
hudud	Specific Islamic criminal punishments
ijma	Community consensus as a tool of modifying and interpreting Islamic law
ijtihad	The practice of informed interpretation, another tool for establishing and modifying correct Islamic practice
Khilafa	Another spelling for *Caliphate*
kufr	Non-Islamic disbelief

madrassa	Generic term for an Islamic religious school, whether of the traditional nonpolitical variety or as a politicized source of radical fundamentalist indoctrination
mullah	An Islamic preacher, regardless of the level of training and education
Quran	The Islamic holy book
sharia	Also commonly spelled *shariah* or *shariat;* the entire body of Islamic law and guidance, based on the Quran, hadith, and scholarly judgments and open to selective use and interpretation
Shi'a Islam	Literally, *faction* or *party;* a dissident version of Islam that began with a dispute over the leadership succession shortly after the death of Muhammad and then developed further doctrinal and political differences vis-à-vis orthodox, Sunni Islam
Sufisim	Islamic mysticism, either in its variant as a populist folk religion or organized in Sufi religious orders
Sunni Islam	The orthodox version of Islam adhered to by the overwhelming majority, although Shi'a Islam is dominant in some countries and regions
sunnah	The body of tradition complementing the Quran
sura	A section or verse of the Quran and the organizing principle structuring the revelations
Ulama	Body of scholars, scholarly community
ummah	The community of believers
Wahhabi	An extremist, puritanical, and aggressive form of Islamic fundamentalism founded in the 18th century and adopted by the house of Saud; disrespecting other versions of Islam, including Sufi Islam, Shi'a Islam, and moderate Islam in general as incorrect aberrations of the true religion. Its expansionist ambitions are heavily funded by the Saudi government.

Chapter One

MAPPING THE ISSUES: AN INTRODUCTION TO THE RANGE OF THOUGHT IN CONTEMPORARY ISLAM

The notion that the outside world should try to encourage a moderate, democratic interpretation and presentation of Islam has been in circulation for some decades but gained great urgency after September 11, 2001.

There is broad agreement that this is a constructive approach. Islam is an important religion with enormous political and societal influence; it inspires a variety of ideologies and political actions, some of which are dangerous to global stability; and it therefore seems sensible to foster the strains within it that call for a more moderate, democratic, peaceful, and tolerant social order. The question is how best to do this. This report identifies a direction.

We begin by setting the scene for the main ideological fissures in the discussion over Islam and society. The second chapter analyzes the pros and cons of supporting different elements within Islam. The final chapter proposes a strategy.

Immediately following September 11, 2001, political leaders and policymakers in the West began to issue statements affirming their conviction that Islam was not to blame for what had happened, that Islam was a positive force in the world, a religion of peace and tolerance. They spoke in mosques, held widely publicized meetings with Muslim clerics, invited mullahs to open public events, and inserted Quranic suras into their own speeches.

In a typical formulation, for example, President Bush asserted that "Islam is a faith that brings comfort to a billion people around the world" and that "has made brothers and sisters of every race. It's a faith based upon love, not hate" (Bush, 2002).

This approach has not been unique to the United States but is also prevalent in Europe, where it led some commentators to note sarcastically that the political leadership "collectively appears to have acquired an instant postgraduate degree in Islamic studies, enabling them to lecture the population concerning the true nature of Islam" (Heitmeyer, 2001).

In part, this demonstrative public embracing of Islam by opinion leaders and politicians had a domestic rationale: Western leaders were attempting to prevent a backlash that might have inspired acts of violence and hostility aimed at their respective Muslim minorities. In addition, there were at least two foreign policy motivations, one short term and the other longer term. In the short run, the goal was to make it politically possible for Muslim governments to support the effort against terrorism by detaching the issue of terrorism from the issue of Islam. In the longer run, the Western leaders were attempting to create an image, a vision, that would facilitate the better integration of Islamic political actors and states into the modern international system.

The academic community quickly joined in, trying to make the case that Islam was at a minimum compatible with, if indeed it did not demand, moderation, tolerance, diversity, and democracy. In his introduction to Abdulaziz Sachedina's *The Islamic Roots of Democratic Pluralism*, Joseph Montville expresses the purpose of such studies and the motivation of the Center for Strategic and International Studies in funding this one,

> We knew that, like every great world religion, Islam embraced certain universal human values that could be recognized and accepted as the basis of community by non-Muslims . . . Prof. Sachedina . . . knew he could highlight those parts of the Koran . . . that emphasized the dignity of the individual, freedom of conscience, and God's love for all creatures, People of the Book and even people without a book. (Sachedina, 2001, p. 1)

And the author himself explains,

> This work undertakes to map some of the most important political concepts in Islam that advance better human relationships, both within and between nations. It aims at *uncovering* normative aspects of Muslim religious formulations and specifying their application in diverse cultures to suggest their critical relevance to the pluralistic world order of the 21st century. . . . The goal here is not to glorify the Muslim past but to remember it, retrace its path, interpret it, reconstruct it and make it relevant to the present. (Sachedina, 2001, p. 1; emphasis added)

However, even as one group of authors was seeking to "highlight" one set of values to be found in the Quran and tradition, other authors were successfully finding and energetically publicizing quite another set of values.

Even as liberal scholars within and outside the Muslim world were gathering intellectual arguments that supported liberal, tolerant Islam, the terrorists were making equal reference to Islam, asserting that their mission and methods were mandated directly by their religion. The celebratory tone taken in some Islamic communities following the attacks soberingly showed that this view was shared by a certain—and not a small—segment of the Muslim public. Even a year after the event, radical clerics meeting in London to celebrate the September 11 attacks averred in their press conference that these had been an exercise in "just retribution" and thus a proper Islamic act (Bowcott, 2002).

Western leaders and supportive governments in the Muslim world have tried hard to detach the terrorists' goals from Islam; the radicals are equally determined to keep the issues joined.[1]

For many Western opinion leaders, the goal of opposing terrorists, of preventing the conflict from turning into a "clash of religions," and of discrediting the radicals' interpretation of Islam, made it seem all the more advisable to support the more benign strains within Islam—but which ones, exactly, and with what concrete goal in mind? Identifying the elements that should be supported, choosing appropriate methods, and defining the goals of such support is difficult.

It is no easy matter to transform a major world religion. If "nation-building" is a daunting task, "religion-building" is immeasurably more perilous and complex. Islam is neither a homogeneous entity nor a simple system. Many extraneous issues and problems have become entangled with religion, and many of the political actors in the region deliberately seek to "Islamize" the debate in a way that they think will further their goals.

THE SETTING: SHARED PROBLEMS, DIFFERENT ANSWERS

Islam's current crisis has two main components: The Islamic world has been marked by a long period of backwardness and comparative powerlessness; many different solutions, such as nationalism, pan-Arabism, Arab socialism, and Islamic revolution, have been attempted without success;[2] and this has led to frustration and anger. At the same time, the Islamic world has fallen out of step with contemporary global culture, as well as moving increasingly to the margins of the global economy.

Muslims disagree on what to do about this, on what has caused it, and on what their societies ultimately should look like. We can distinguish four essential positions, as the following paragraphs describe.

The **fundamentalists**[3] put forth an aggressive, expansionist version of Islam that does not shy away from violence. They want to gain political power and then to impose strict public observance of Islam, as they themselves define it, forcibly on as broad a population worldwide as possible. Their unit of reference

---

[1]For example, in a speech on September 21, 2002, the head of Pakistan's fundamentalist Jamaat-e-Islami party, Qazi Hussain Ahmed, reiterated that the United States was the "worst enemy of Islam" and considered "Islam as the main hurdle in the way of achieving its ulterior motives in the world." The so-called alliance against terrorism was in reality an anti-Islamic struggle aimed at "eliminating Muslim countries from the globe."

[2]See, especially, Roy (1994); Tibi (1988); Ajami (1981); and Rejwan (1998).

[3]The term *Islamist* is being variously used by different authors to describe either the fundamentalists or the traditionalists. To avoid confusion, it will not be used in this report .

is not the nation-state or the ethnic group, but the Muslim community, the *ummah*; gaining control of particular Islamic countries can be a step on this path but is not the main goal.

We can distinguish two strands within fundamentalism. One, which is grounded in theology and tends to have some roots in one or another kind of religious establishment, we will refer to as the *scriptural fundamentalists*. On the Shi'a side, this group includes most of the Iranian revolutionaries and, as one Sunni manifestation, the Saudi-based Wahhabis. The Kaplan congregation, active among Western diaspora Turks and in Turkey, is another example.

The *radical fundamentalists*, the second strand, are much less concerned with the literal substance of Islam, with which they take considerable liberties either deliberately or because of ignorance of orthodox Islamic doctrine. They usually do not have any "institutional" religious affiliations but tend to be eclectic and autodidactic in their knowledge of Islam. Al Qaeda, the Afghan Taliban, Hizb-ut-Tahrir, and a large number of other Islamic radical movements and diffuse groups worldwide belong to this category.

The fundamentalists do not merely approve of the Islamic practices of the past. More significantly, they expand on them, applying some of the more stringent rules more rigorously than the original Islamic community ever did, exercising an arbitrary selectivity that allows them to ignore or drop more egalitarian, progressive, tolerant aspects of the Quran and the sunnah, and inventing some new rules of their own. This is particularly true of the radical fundamentalists.

Not all fundamentalists embrace or even endorse terrorism, at least not the indiscriminate type of terrorism that targets civilians and often kills Muslims along with the "enemy," but fundamentalism as a whole is incompatible with the values of civil society and the Western vision of civilization, political order, and society.

The **traditionalists** are also divided into two distinct groups: conservative traditionalists and reformist traditionalists. The distinction is significant.

Conservative traditionalists believe that Islamic law and tradition ought to be rigorously and literally followed, and they see a role for the state and for the political authorities in encouraging or at least facilitating this. However, they do not generally favor violence and terrorism.

Historically, they have grown accustomed to operating under changing political circumstances, and this has led them to concentrate their efforts on the daily life of the society, where they try to have as much influence and control as they can, even when the government is not Islamic. In the social realm, their goal is to preserve orthodox norms and values and conservative behavior to the fullest extent possible. The temptations and the pace of modern life are seen as posing a major threat to this. Their posture is one of resistance to change.

Additionally, there are often important differences between conservative traditionalists who live in the Islamic world or in the Third World generally and those who live in the West. Being an essentially moderate position, traditionalism tends to be adaptive to its environment. Thus, conservative traditionalists who live in traditional societies are likely to accept practices that are prevalent in such societies, such as child marriage, and to be less educated and less able to distinguish local traditions and customs from actual Islamic doctrine. Those who live in the West have absorbed more-modern views on these issues and tend to be better educated and more linked to the transnational discourse on issues of orthodoxy.

Reformist traditionalists think that, to remain viable and attractive throughout the ages, Islam has to be prepared to make some concessions in the literal application of orthodoxy. They are prepared to discuss reforms and reinterpretations. Their posture is one of cautious adaptation to change, being flexible on the letter of the law to conserve the spirit of the law.

The **modernists** actively seek far-reaching changes to the current orthodox understanding and practice of Islam. They want to eliminate the harmful ballast of local and regional tradition that has, over the centuries, intertwined itself with Islam. They further believe in the historicity of Islam, i.e., that Islam as it was practiced in the days of the Prophet reflected eternal truths as well as historical circumstances that were appropriate to that time but are no longer valid. They think it is possible to identify an "essential core" of Islamic belief; further, they believe that this core will not only remain undamaged but in fact will be strengthened by changes, even very substantial changes, that reflect changing times, social conditions, and historical circumstances.

The things that modernists value and admire most about Islam tend to be quite different and more abstract than the things the fundamentalists and the traditionalists value. Their core values—the primacy of the individual conscience and a community based on social responsibility, equality, and freedom—are easily compatible with modern democratic norms.

The **secularists** believe that religion should be a private matter separate from politics and the state and that the main challenge lies in preventing transgressions in either direction. The state should not interfere in the individual exercise of religion, but equally, religious customs must be in conformity with the law of the land and with human rights. The Turkish Kemalists, who placed religion under the firm control of the state, represent the laicist model in Islam.

These positions should be thought of as representing segments on a continuum, rather than distinct categories. There are no clear boundaries between them, so that some traditionalists overlap with the fundamentalists; the most modernist of the traditionalists are almost modernists; and the most extreme modernists are similar to secularists.

Each of these outlined positions takes a characteristic stance on key issues of controversy in the contemporary Islamic debate. And their "rules of evidence" for defending these positions are also distinct, as sketched in Table 1 (starting on page 8).

In the contemporary Islamic struggle, "lifestyle" issues are the field on which the contending positions try to stake their claims and that they use to signal their control. Doctrine is territory and is being fought over. This explains the prominence of such issues in an ideological and political contest.

The utility of "mapping" the views of the various Islamic positions is that, on issues of doctrine and lifestyle, they adhere to fairly distinct and reliable platforms, which define their identity and serve as identifiers toward like-minded others—a kind of "passport."

Thus, while it is possible for groups to dissimulate concerning their attitude to violence, to avoid prosecution and sanctions, it is not really possible for them to distort or deny their views on key value and lifestyle issues. These are what define them and attract new members.

Conservative traditionalists accept the correctness of past practices, even when they conflict with today's norms and values, on the principle that the original Islamic community represents the absolute and eternal ideal, but they no longer necessarily attempt to reinstate all of the practices. Often, however, their reason for this is not that they would not like to do it, but that they assess it to be temporarily or permanently unrealistic to do so. Reformist traditionalists reinterpret, rebut, or evade practices that seem problematic in today's world. Modernists see the same practices as part of a changing and changeable historical context; they do not regard the original Islamic community or the early years of Islam as something that one would necessarily wish to reproduce today. Secularists prohibit the practices that conflict with modern norms and laws and ignore the others as belonging to the private sphere of individuals.

Secularists do not concern themselves with what Islam might or might not require. Moderate secularists want the state to guarantee people's right to practice their faith, while ensuring that religion remains a private matter and does not violate any standards of human rights or civil law. Radical secularists, including communists and laicists, oppose religion altogether.

Conservative traditionalists seek guidance from conventional Islamic sources: the Quran, the sunnah, Islamic law, fatwas, and the religious opinions of respected scholars. Reformist traditionalists use the same sources but tend to be more inventive and more aggressive in exploring alternative interpretations. They are aware of the conflicts between modernity and Islam and want to reduce them to keep Islam viable into the future. They seek to reinterpret traditional content, to find ways around the restrictions or rulings that trouble them or stand in the way of desired changes or that harm the image of Islam in the eyes of the rest of the world.

There are ironic similarities in the way radical fundamentalists and modernists approach the issue of change. In keeping with convention, they both refer to the Quran, sunnah, law, fatwas, and authorities (of course, choosing different selections from each). But ultimately, both positions are guided by their respective visions of the ideal Islamic society. Each feels authorized to define and interpret the individual rules and laws in keeping with that vision. Obviously, this gives them a lot more freedom to maneuver than the traditionalists have.

Fundamentalists have as their goal an ascetic, highly regimented, hierarchical society in which all members follow the requirements of Islamic ritual strictly, in which immorality is prevented by separating the sexes, which in turn is achieved by banishing women from the public domain, and in which life is visibly and constantly infused by religion. It is totalitarian in its negation of a private sphere, instead believing that it is the task of state authorities to compel the individual to adhere to proper Islamic behavior anywhere and everywhere. And ideally, it wants this system—which it believes to be the only rightful one—to expand until it controls the entire world and everyone is a Muslim.

Modernists envision a society in which individuals express their piety in a way each finds personally meaningful, decide most moral matters and lifestyle issues on the basis of their own consciences, seek to lead ethical lives out of inner conviction rather than external compulsion, and base their political system on principles of justice and equality. This system should coexist peacefully with other orders and religions. The modernists find concepts within Islamic orthodoxy that support the right of Muslims, as individuals and as communities, to make changes and revisions even to basic laws and texts.

When a question arises that is not covered in Islamic orthodox texts, or when it is but they do not like the answer, fundamentalists and modernists both refer instead to their ideal vision and then innovate a solution. Since innovation is not generally accepted in Islam, they both define it as something else.

Modernists speak of "faith-based objections" to specific aspects of Islam, of the "good of the community" as a value that overrides even the Quran, of "community consensus" (*ijma*) that legitimizes even radical change.[4]

Radical fundamentalists reclaim *ijtihad*, the controversial practice of interpretation, or refer mysteriously to "higher criteria." No traditionalist would ever argue that orthodox content of the Quran or the hadith can be "technically

---

[4]See, for example, El Fadl (2001).

Table 1

"Marker Issues" and the Major Ideological Positions in Islam

	Radical Fundamentalists	Scriptural Fundamentalists	Conservative Traditionalists
Democracy	A wrongful creed. Sovereignty and the right to legislate belong to God alone.	Islam is a form of democracy. The West has no right to define what democracy should look like, and the Islamic form is superior because it rests on the only correct and perfect religion.	There is some room for democratic instruments in the interpretation of Islamic practice, in community life and in certain sectors of public life.
Human rights, individual liberties	Erroneous decadent concepts that lead to corruption. The full imposition of shari'a creates a good and just society.	Humans need guidance and control, but these must be reasonable and fair, as set down in sunnah and the Quran.	Islam, properly lived, provides the optimum setting for humans. Equality and freedom are wrong concepts; Islam instead gives everyone their due in accord with their station and nature.
Polygamy	Is permitted and there is nothing wrong with it. Superior to Western immorality and serial divorce.	Permitted as a way to enhance public and individual morality, but not for self-indulgence.	Permitted under certain circumstances, including when all wives are treated equally, as the Quran requires, and only if local law permits it. But monogamy is superior.
Islamic criminal penalties, including flogging, amputations, stoning for adultery	An excellent way to provide swift, deterrent justice.	Just and correct, but may have to be implemented with discretion as it is no longer quite in line with world public opinion and can thus be detrimental to the image of Islamic states.	Should be used if the country follows shari'a law, which Muslim countries ought to do. Severe shari'a punishment has good deterrent effect but was intended to be mitigated by mercy, forgiveness, rehabilitation efforts, and strict rules of evidence.

Table 1—Continued

Reformist Traditionalists	Modernists	Mainstream Secularists	Radical Secularists
Islam has at heart been democratic from its inception; the community of believers is sovereign, and even the earliest leaders were chosen by democratic means.	Islam contains democratic concepts that need to be brought to the forefront.	Democracy is primary; Islam must (and can) bring itself into line with it and with the separation of church and state.	Social justice is more important than democracy.
Properly interpreted and applied, Islam guarantees human rights and such liberties as are actually good for a person, not false ones that lead the person on a wrongful path.	Islam contains the basic concepts of human rights and individual freedom, including the freedom to do wrong.	Islam can attempt to guide the behavior of those who adhere to it, in their private lives, where they can give up some of their freedoms if they choose. However, in overall social and political life, human rights are paramount and universal.	Equality and justice are more important than individual liberties.
Permitted in societies that legally allow it, but it should be the exception, and the agreement of the first wife should be obtained. In general, monogamy is thought better, but a defensive traditionalist position shares the fundamentalist argument that polygamy is better than Western sexual anarchy.	Not permitted. An archaic practice, such as those found in other religions, that was considered less than ideal even at the time, and there is evidence that Muhammad was trying to abolish it.	Against modern laws and accepted practice; therefore ,not permitted.	Not permitted, although some would also consider monogamy to be a hypocritical bourgeois concept.
Should not be used. The most severe punishments were never intended to be implemented except in very rare cases; they have been misapplied and misunderstood and often have no real Quranic basis.	Should not be used. These punishments are either archaic, in line with the common practice of their era but no longer appropriate, or they were wrongly interpreted in the first place.	Not legal in most countries and not in keeping with international human rights or contemporary norms; therefore ,cannot be applied.	Religion is a fallacy; therefore, religious laws can never be legitimate.

Table 1—Continued

	Radical Fundamentalists	Scriptural Fundamentalists	Conservative Traditionalists
Hijab	Women must wear Islamic garments, usually to cover all but the face and hands but, in some places, also to conceal the face and hands. In the diaspora, a headscarf is the acceptable minimum. It is society's job to make sure women adhere to this rule through persuasion, pressure, education, and coercion. Men must also conform visually, usually by wearing a beard and short hair.	Islamic covering is required for women and should be coercively enforced.	Hijab is preferable. It can be enforced by family, peer, and community pressure. Not all traditionalists agree that real coercion is also acceptable. Both genders should dress modestly. Traditionalists in conservative societies: Women should cover everything but the hands and face. Traditionalists in the West and in modern societies: The scarf and long clothing is enough.
Beating of wives	Allowed and useful to control behavior of women and to maintain hierarchy in the family.	The Quran allows it, but it is permissible only as a well-intentioned pedagogical intervention to correct the behavior of an errant wife for her own good and that of the family and society.	Same as scriptural fundamentalists.
Status of minorities	Tolerated, but they cannot practice their own religion or culture in any visible way. They are inferior, and thus it is acceptable to discriminate against them. It is best if they convert.	Tolerated, as long as they do not engage in missionary activities.	Tolerated and should be treated decently and allowed to practice their religions and cultures, unless they are contrary to Islamic morality and law.
Islamic state	An Islamic state should be global and supranational. It should guide all conduct, policing such things as prayer attendance, beard length, clothing. Any matter not explicitly covered by a rule requires the advice of a religious authority.	Islam is possible on the basis of individual states, although a supranational ummah remains the ideal.	An Islamic state is best, because people can then most fully exercise their religion. Next best is to live immersed in an Islamic community, doing as told by your elders, family, and the community's religious leaders.

Table 1—Continued

Reformist Traditionalists	Modernists	Mainstream Secularists	Radical Secularists
Women should dress modestly; the definition of that depends on where the traditionalist lives and ranges from all-but-face-and-hands to the scarf to no scarf, as long as the body is not provocatively displayed.	Islam does not require women to wear any sort of veil or head covering. There is no textual substantiation for such rules. It is up to the individual to decide what to wear. Women should not be held responsible for men's possible licentious thoughts, since the Quran clearly instructs men to "lower their gaze," i.e., not to stare salaciously at women, and vice versa.	Muslims can wear whatever they want, but public schools and professions where it would impinge on performance or the rights of others can, if they see fit, prohibit the wearing of hijab, scarves, etc.	Hijab is a symbol of backwardness, and women should not want to wear it, let alone be pressured or forced into doing so.
No longer allowed, and the religious basis for it is questionable anyway. The Quranic passage permitting it has been challenged, and many hadiths reflect Muhammad's disapproval of it.	Not allowed, based on incorrect religious interpretation, and clearly against the spirit of Islamic concept of marriage and gender relations.	Not allowed, because it is illegal, and against contemporary norms and human rights.	Reflects archaic notion of wives as property, and so is not allowed.
Tolerated, and they should be well treated, encouraged to practice their religions and cultures if possible, and should be engaged in dialogue.	Should be treated on equal footing.	Assimilation into secular society is best.	Most of these affiliations represent false consciousness.
An Islamic state is best. Barring that, individual religious studies are important, backed by support of a like-minded community and religious experts to give guidance.	Islam was not meant to be a state but a code and guiding philosophy for life. The individual holds ultimate responsibility for his or her behavior and decisions, in the context of an ever-changing, vibrant community of thinking and questioning rational individuals.	Islam is a religion and thus a private matter; the state has the obligation to allow it, but Muslims have the obligation to obey civil law and local custom and to adapt to the age in which they live.	Religion is a retrograde force in society and should be abolished.

Table 1—Continued

	Radical Fundamentalists	Scriptural Fundamentalists	Conservative Traditionalists
Public participation of women	There must be maximum separation of women from men. Women should be excluded from the public domain to the fullest extent possible.	Iranian style Shi'a fundamentalism: Women should play an active role in society and political life, but there must be strict segregation, and the highest offices in justice and government are reserved for men. Sunni: Governance is the domain of men. Women can be active in fields related to children and social matters.	Women are responsible for the family; if that is completely taken care of, they can be active in certain professions and in community and public life but in a subsidiary function.
Jihad	There are different levels of jihad, but armed struggle for the establishment of a universal and worldwide Islamic order is incumbent upon anyone physically capable of participating. This can take the form of classical warfare or of terrorism and insurgency.	The definition of jihad varies from person to person. For women, childbirth is a form of jihad. Jihad includes the struggle for personal spiritual betterment. For some groups under some circumstances, it includes armed struggle, including terrorism.	Jihad is primarily the struggle for personal moral betterment, but it encompasses war on behalf of Islam when necessary and appropriate.
Sources	The Quran, sunnah, charismatic leaders, radical authors, with all details subordinated to the broad vision of a rigorously pious, Islamic society.	The Quran, sunnah, Islamic philosophy, science, scholarly interpretation, and charismatic leaders.	The Quran, sunnah, local custom and tradition, and the opinions of local mullahs

Table 1—Continued

Reformist Traditionalists	Modernists	Mainstream Secularists	Radical Secularists
Women are responsible first for the family, which is a very important role, but they can also take part in economic and public and political life, where they bring an added ,female, perspective. They can hold high office as women did during Muhammad's time. In the view of some, this excludes the position of head of state.	Family and community are important in Islam, and both genders should take responsibility there. All professions and all types of public and political offices are open to women. This was the case in Muhammad's time, when women even fought in his army, were appointed by him to be judges, and even led men in prayer ,and is certainly the case today.	Discrimination is illegal; equal rights and opportunities are the desirable norm.	All forms of inequality should be eliminated.
Jihad is a struggle for personal moral betterment. Only in very exceptional circumstances, such as a life or death struggle for the survival of the faith when attacked, does it include the obligation to engage in "holy war."	Jihad is a symbolic term referring to personal spiritual development.	Jihad as holy war is a historical reference. In the contemporary world, it refers to spiritual development, but since it is liable to be misunderstood, it is better not to use the term.	Fighting wars on the grounds of religion and religious differences is completely archaic and wrong.
The Quran, sunnah, the guidance of a wide assortment of scholars (including secular philosophers), modern laws and ethical codes, and community consensus.	The Quran, sunnah, historical and contemporary philosophy, and modern laws and ethical codes, in an effort to understand the essential spirit of Islam in the context of the present age.	Civil law, international human rights, and the philosophical underpinnings of secularism.	Specific ideology of the group or movement.

defensible" but still be contrary to the "spirit of the Prophet's tradition" and therefore may be abandoned.

The next section illustrates how the positions define their views on the key issues we have identified.

In terms of its public manifestation, the division between the contemporary positions in Islam plays itself out in regard to issues of lifestyle and values. In some ways, this is what marks it most clearly as a religion-based dispute: Distinctions that may appear relatively minor in the grand scheme of things take on enormous importance because they signify allegiance or nonallegiance, victory or stalemate. The obvious example is the "head scarf." It is important for outside actors to keep this in mind.

When U.S. government agencies appear to endorse the head scarf, for example, considering this to be a minor matter of preference in dress code that cheaply enables them to signal tolerance, they are in fact unwittingly taking a major stand on a central, wildly contested symbolic issue. They are aligning themselves with the extreme end of the spectrum, with the fundamentalists and the conservative traditionalists, against the reformist traditionalists, the modernists, and the secularists.

POSITIONS ON KEY ISSUES

Democracy and Human Rights

Illustrations of the radical fundamentalist position on issues of political doctrine can readily be found in print and online in the publications of Hezbi-Islami and Hizb-ut-Tahrir, to name only two sources:

According to Hezbi-Islami, parliaments and other democratic institutions are

> clear and obvious forms of disbelief, and of *shirk*, or setting up rivals to Allah (by ascribing legislative power to people) and an unforgivable sin, and a contradiction of the purpose of creation.[5]

The goal is to impose the correct order, that of Islam, over all others. According to Green (1994),

> This is not a confrontation of civilizations, nor is it a clash of cultures. Islam does not oppose the West, or anyone else, because of revenge over past hostilities, out of a desire to restore injured pride or because of the desire to amass their wealth and lands. The fight is for one purpose only and that is to establish

---

[5]Note that all our quotations from and citations of online materials reflect the content as it existed between January and September 2002. Some of these texts have been changed or modified since then, though not substantially.

the religion of Islam in its totality . . . . Jihad has three characteristics. The first stage is to acquire the correct creed and to remove from one's self all doubts and misconceptions . . . The second stage is . . . releasing the lands of the Muslims from the control of their enemies . . . The final stage is that of fighting in order to open the path for establishing Allah's rule in the land of the unbelievers.

Similarly, Hizb-ut-Tahrir describes itself as "a political party whose ideology is Islam, so politics is its work and Islam is its ideology . . . to restore the Khilafah [the Caliphate]" As concerns governance, "the constitution and canons must be Islamic," and it cannot be

republican. The republican system is based on the democratic system, which is a system of Kufr (disbelief) . . . In [the Islamic system] the sovereignty is for the Shari'a and not for the Ummah. The legislator is Allah. The Khaleefa only possesses the right to adopt rules for the constitution and canons from the Book of Allah and the Sunnah of His Messenger. Therefore, it is not permitted to say that the system of Islam is a republican system or to talk of an Islamic republic . . . .[6]

Polygamy

Fundamentalists accept polygamy. The Taliban reintroduced the practice in Afghanistan, where it had mostly fallen into disuse. Child marriage is often a corollary of polygamy, and it is prevalent in societies that fundamentalists control but also in some places conservative traditionalists control. The Taliban and Afghanistan-based al Qaeda also practiced forced marriages, which the Quran accepts in the context of war.

Reformist traditionalists and **conservative traditionalists** who live in the West or in countries that do not endorse this practice do not support the active practice of polygamy. Some of them disavow it only because they believe that Muslims must respect the laws of whatever country they live in. They have no objection to Muslim men who, although they already have a wife at home, wish to marry a second one in the foreign country they have come to for work or study, and Islamic expatriate Web sites offer advice to prospective brides who find themselves having second thoughts.[7] Traditionalists who are closer to the modernist end of the spectrum, and those who believe this issue not to be worth the scorn and disapproval it inspires in outsiders, genuinely oppose polygamy. However, there is no doubt that the Quran allows it and that Muhammad and the early leaders of Islam practiced it. Therefore, being tradi-

---

[6]"Definition" and "Party Culture," on Hizb-ut-Tahrir's official Web site.

[7]Note that all our citations of online publications and Web sites reflect the content as it existed between January and September 2002. Some of these texts have been changed or modified since then, though not substantially.

tionalists, they are unable to disavow it and, in fact, feel obliged to defend it. To this purpose, they generally put forward one or more of the following arguments to make it more palatable to modern audiences:

They point out that Muhammad was monogamous during the lifetime of his first wife, Khadija, during which Islam was first revealed to him. This, they say, should therefore be taken as the ideal condition for Muslims to emulate.

They say that Muhammad's multiple marriages were largely made for alliances and were either political or charitable rather than being personal. These traditionalists point out that some were probably marriages in name only, designed to cement a political alliance or care for a friend's widow.[8] In fact, they argue, polygamy in the early Muslim community was a kind of welfare project, a response to the shortage of men that war had caused, which led to a surplus of women, including many widows in need of protectors and breadwinners.

It replaced, others assert, the much worse misuse of women in pre-Islamic society, in contrast to which a regulated polygamy limited to only four wives who had to be treated equally and whose economic and legal status was guaranteed was an improvement.

Reformist traditionalists (like fundamentalists) sometimes argue that polygamy can be seen as a convenience for women, who can share child-raising and domestic chores and thereby free their time for jobs and other interests. Also, they assert, the practice is superior to what has emerged in the West. The high divorce rate in Western industrial society, after all, is really just a form of serial polygamy. Since it includes abandonment, it is especially hurtful to the women and children involved, while the Islamic approach entitles the displaced wife to a lifetime of equal financial, emotional, and (theoretically) sexual disbursements.

Women who find the practice personally offensive are legally entitled to add a stipulation to their marriage contract that will prevent their husband from taking additional wives, these traditionalists note.

A somewhat laborious argument that traditionalists frequently use is that the injunction to treat all wives equally was really just a kind of divine sleight-of-hand. Since it is impossible to do this, as the Quran itself elsewhere observes, the injunction in fact nullifies polygamy.

A typical text might argue as follows (Maqsood, 1994b, pp. 182–183):

> The Prophet remained monogamous throughout the 24 years of his marriage to Khadijah; after her death he married the widow Sawdah and was engaged to his friend's daughter, Aisha; and after the deaths of so many Muslims in battle the

---

[8]For one of many refutations of this version, see Calislar (1999).

permission to marry up to four wives was given to Muslim men. The Prophet himself had special dispensation and married 13 women in total, all except Aisha being widows or divorcees needing care . . .

Polygamy is also allowed if a man's wife becomes so physically ill that she is no longer able to look after him or the family, or if she becomes mentally ill. Should a man be expected to live for the rest of his life without any sexual comfort, or should he divorce the unfortunate wife, or should he marry another?

(The author—a woman—does not explain why the reverse occurrence should not therefore authorize the woman to take more than one husband.)

Similarly, in his book *Islam Today*, which received the *Los Angeles. Times* award for best nonfiction book of the year, U.S. reformist traditionalist Akbar Ahmed (2001, p. 152) writes,

There is another idea about family life that is difficult to lay to rest in the West. It is of Islam as a man's paradise with every man possessing at least four wives . . . . The Quran has clearly given permission for men to marry more than once, and in certain circumstances this is a social necessity: . . . "marry such women as seem good to you, two, three or four" (4:3). But in the next line the Quran lays down a clause: "If you think you will not act justly, then one." This is a stringent condition making it difficult for a person to marry more than once. Indeed the Quran itself says that polygamy is not possible: "You will never manage to deal equitably with women no matter how hard you try" (4:129). The true spirit of the Quran thus appears to be monogamy . . . . None the less Muslims are not apologetic or defensive about polygamy . . . .

Modernists do not need to engage in such elaborations. They simply point to the fact that "changing times" bring changing customs and moralities. What was acceptable hundreds of years ago is no longer considered acceptable today—and of course the Quran was ambivalent about it even then. Instead of focusing on specifics that are no longer relevant in the entirely different setting of a modern urban world, one should concentrate on the essence of the Prophet's teachings and his example. One will then find that he strove toward ever greater equality, justice, and harmony as the guiding principles of social interaction, that he was a social reformer. Therefore, introducing reforms into society is in keeping with the spirit of Islam.

Criminal Punishments, Islamic Justice

Fundamentalists and many conservative traditionalists argue for the deterrent value of Islam's severe criminal penalties. This is usually not true of reformist traditionalists, however. As traditionalists, they do not feel able to criticize or deny the rules. Instead, they look for ways around them.

In the case of theft, for example, some do this by arguing that most instances of that crime fall outside the strict legal definition of the circumstances that would warrant amputation. If poverty, material need, hunger, or the desire to provide for one's family are present as a motive, they claim, the thief is exonerated—society is to be blamed for the crime, not the person who was forced by adverse circumstances to commit it. If, on the other hand, the theft is completely frivolous, it clearly constitutes a mental disturbance, which again is a mitigating circumstance that excuses the perpetrator from such a severe punishment. (See, for example, Maqsood, 1994b, p. 137.)

How Muslim countries resolve such dilemmas mirrors the forces active within them. Pakistan, for example, is home to a vocal and politically potent fundamentalist segment; it also has a significant traditionalist population; and politically, it wishes to affiliate itself with the modern international community. How can the country reconcile these goals on the issue of Islamic criminal justice? Abandoning shari'a law would alienate the fundamentalists and portions of the traditionalists, but amputating hands and stoning adulterers would lead to international condemnation and alienate domestic modernists and some traditionalists. The solution: Impose shari'a sentences but do not carry them out. (See, for example, Reuters, 2002.)

We can also apply the reverse approach, deducing a country's goals from the policy it chooses on shari'a law. If a country not only pays lip service to shari'a law but actually imposes the consequent sentences, we can conclude that it is interested only in the audience of fundamentalists and conservative traditionalists and has no desire to align itself with the modern democratic world.

Besides amputations of the hands and, in the cases of repeat offenders, also the feet of thieves, shari'a law imposes the death sentence for adultery and flogging for fornication. This is not controversial among fundamentalists or the conservative traditionalists closest to them—but it should be, because there is significant ambiguity in the Quran on this issue. Concerning the treatment of adulterous women, the text says to "call in four witnesses from among yourselves against them; if they testify to their guilt confine them to their houses till death overtakes them or till Allah finds another way for them."

This can be interpreted to mean that the woman should be immured or walled in until she dies of suffocation, or starvation, but equally, it can be taken to require her solitary lifelong confinement until her natural death. There is no reported instance of this punishment in either interpretation being implemented in any Muslim country, even though the Quran is unequivocal in ordering it. Instead, women (and men) deemed guilty of adultery have variously been beheaded, stoned, or shot, with stoning the most common method.

The more commonly seized-upon escape clause for reformist traditionalists and conservative traditionalists refers to the rules of evidence. An adultery charge requires four Muslim witnesses. The text itself, as we saw, does not specify what exactly these witnesses ought to have seen. Orthodox scholars generally say that they must have seen the actual act of adultery, not just circumstantial evidence leading them to believe that it had likely taken place. This clearly stacks the deck significantly in favor of the defendant.

Fundamentalists are not usually constrained by that rule, which shows that they are well outside the bounds of orthodoxy. There were, for example, no witnesses at all in the case of the Nigerian woman recently sentenced to death for adultery. In her case, the fact that she had given birth to a child, although she was not married, sufficed as evidence. Neither the Quran nor any of the thousands of hadiths mentions such a conclusion, although surely such a circumstance must also have occurred at some point during those years. If anything, this judgment contradicts the Quranic injunction that a woman should "never be made to suffer on account of her child." It is not difficult to extend that injunction to mean that a woman probably should not be executed on account of her child.

But fundamentalists, as noted earlier, do not feel constrained by the literal substance of Islam. Nowhere was this more evident than with the Taliban. They executed women by shooting them—a penalty certainly not in keeping with the literal law of Islam, which originated before the age of guns. The Taliban also executed homosexuals, inventing in that case both the death penalty and the means of executing it: tying them to a wall and running a bulldozer over them to crush them to death (see Ahmad Rashid, 2000, and Amnesty International, 1999). The Quran says: "If two men among you commit indecency punish them both. If they repent and mend their ways, let them be" (4:13). It does not mention the nature of the punishment, but bulldozers cannot have been involved, and it does not seem likely that, given the alternative, the Taliban's victims were given the option of "repenting" and refused it.

Shari'a law prescribes flogging as a penalty for various offenses, such as the consumption of alcohol. International public opinion no longer considers this to be a civilized form of punishment. Again, traditionalists cannot override the fact that Islamic law clearly calls for this punishment. They can only seek arguments to make it somehow more palatable.

The case reformist traditionalist author Ruqaiyyah Maqsood (1994a, p. 138) makes is typical:

> There are numerous rules governing the administration of Islamic flogging; it is not just a savage beating inflicted capriciously . . . . It has to be done with control, in accord with justice, and in the kindest possible way in the circumstances, following a long list of stipulations, including deferment when someone is sick, not to touch face, head or private parts, women to be fully clothed and allowed to sit, not to be done on days of extreme heat or cold, and so forth.

As with adultery, one can also minimize the chances that the undesirable penalty will be applied by adding to the burden of proof. For instance, a number of hadiths discourage believers from spying on each other, denouncing others or trying to find fault with them. These can be used to argue that drinking in the privacy of one's own home should not be punished, since it would not have been discovered in the first place if someone had not first violated the injunction against meddling and spying.

Minorities

The picture that study of the text yields about other monotheistic religions is mixed. The Quran contains many hostile, incendiary passages about Jews and Christians, but it also contains some conciliatory ones. This has been explained in reference to historic circumstances—the original Islamic community was at war with these groups.

In general, non-Muslims living under Muslim control are supposed to be permitted to practice their religions without obstacles. Muslim men are even instructed to allow their Jewish or Christian wives to practice their faiths freely. Minorities should be able to have their own courts and apply their own laws in civil matters. Historically, minority communities have often fared relatively well under Islamic empires.

Fundamentalists do not continue this tradition, instead tending to act repressively toward non-Muslims living under their control. Fundamentalist terrorist groups have attacked churches in Pakistan, killing the worshipers. In Saudi Arabia, Christians and Jews may not establish churches or synagogues and may not observe their own religious holidays.

The Taliban imposed its rules on everyone.[9] When the Taliban adopted the Wahhabi religious interpretation that women should not be permitted to drive cars, it also applied to foreign women working with nongovernmental organizations (NGOs). Hindus were excused from the forcibly imposed public prayers but at the expense of stigmatization: They were supposed to wear yellow identifying patches.

Traditionalists tend to be ecumenical, although their goals are to establish an Islamic society and encourage conversion. In theory, this should be accomplished by setting a good example and by persuasion, not by compulsion.

---

[9]The Taliban Ministry for the Propagation of Virtue and Suppression of Vice appears to have not only been copied from but also trained and funded by the Saudi religious police, or *mutaween* (Fisk, 1998).

Women's Dress

On purely objective grounds, it is surprising that the issue of hijab has managed to attain such vast importance, because the Quran very manifestly does not support it. The Quran requires modest dress and modest conduct for both men and women. It does not specify what that means in terms of clothing but cites two guidelines: local custom and the person's station in life, i.e., his or her work. Only a very specific group of women, namely the Prophet's wives, were instructed to cover themselves in the hijab sense of the term. This provision is contained in a late section of the Quran that specifically addresses the ways in which their situation differs from that of other women. They are asked to consider their unusual circumstances and to accept exceptional restrictions—not to remarry after the Prophet dies and to wear special concealing garments—and in return they are promised "double the reward" of ordinary mortals.

Modernists and the more progressive among reformist traditionalists point this out. They also note the explanation given in the Quran and hadith for the rules of dress: Modest people are supposed to avoid attracting special notice. Where it is not the majority dress, hijab accomplishes the opposite. It draws special attention to a woman and causes people to stare at her, the very effect she should be trying to avoid, were she truly modest. Finally, they refer to two basic messages in the Quran: that there should be "no compulsion in religion" and that "God does not desire hardship, but desires ease" for his followers. Pressuring women to wear a certain mode of dress they have not freely chosen, constraining their ability to work, singling them out for hostility or discrimination, causing a negative impact on their comfort and health—none of these are in harmony with that injunction.

Scriptural fundamentalists and traditionalists engage in lengthy debates over the issue of women's dress, weighing the pros and cons of various arguments before coming to some sort of judgment. Web sites in which people narrate the years-long soul-searching they have personally engaged in over this issue are very popular, as are narratives of girls describing why they have decided to wear or not to wear hijab, and pronouncements by numerous religious experts.

Radical fundamentalists ignore the debate; for them, the issue is settled, and hijab is mandatory. One hallmark of radical fundamentalist doctrinal practice is their selectivity. Typically, their publications on this subject will quote the sura urging "believing women to lower their gaze" but will leave out the rest of the sentence, which identically requires "believing men to lower their gaze." However, while the largest part of the burden of maintaining "public morality" falls on women, who must accept restrictive dress and banishment from public space, fundamentalist men are not entirely exempt. As the Australian fundamentalist Web site Nida'ul Islam recommends, all children should be taught to feel uncomfortable in the presence of the opposite sex and embarrassed about their bodies (Islam, 1998):

> We should use the Prophet as an example: Abu Said Al Khudri reported that the Prophet was more shy than a virgin in her own room. (Bukhari) If we instill this into [children] at an early age then, inshallah, whenever they are near the vicinity of the opposite sex, they will feel shy and, therefore, will not act inappropriately.[10]

This premise—that a person who is socialized to feel inhibited and neurotic about sexuality is more likely to act "appropriately" in this sphere is an adult—clearly depends on one's definition of what constitutes appropriate conduct.

In any event, the issue of hijab has become highly politicized. As one expert notes,[11]

> Hijab . . . has become a symbol of traditionalism and fundamentalism. As such it is politicized and used by anti-Western groups from Turkey to Malaysia and throughout the Arab world. Western governments, especially the U.S., should refrain from making any references to "the right of women to wear the hijab" as being a simple democratic right. It is more than this, and the hidden message behind hijab is very dangerous.

Husbands Allowed to Beat Wives

Fundamentalists have no problem with this. In the case of radical fundamentalists, it fits their hierarchical view of society and their ideal of female subordination. Scriptural fundamentalists find it to be in accord with their overall disciplinary approach to human conduct, which includes such institutions as a religious police armed with whips and sticks, patrolling the streets to monitor the length of men's hair, the observance of prayers, the absence of polish on women's fingernails, and the like.

Conservative traditionalists also accept the practice[12] but try to make a distinction between a "benevolent" didactic intervention, employed rarely and

---

[10]Note that the title of the article in which this appears uses *G-B* as a discreet abbreviation for *Girlfriend-Boyfriend*, a relationship apparently too horrible even to spell out. Let it be noted that, on the basis of hadith, one rather gains the impression that Muhammad was relaxed and informal in the presence of women. He liked to socialize with Aisha's friends, stayed in the room when they visited her to play music, joked with women in the neighborhood, and gave advice to women on a variety of quite intimate matters.

[11]Birol Yesilada, personal communication, March 2003.

[12]For example, see Abdur Rahman Doi (2001):

> A refractory wife has no legal right to object to her husband exercising his disciplinary authority. Islamic law, in keeping with most other systems of law (which ones might those be? He does not specify), recognizes the husband's right to discipline his wife for disobedience.

Doi is Director of the Center for Islamic Legal Studies, Ahmadu Bello University, Zaira, Nigeria.

intended to correct the wife's wrongful behavior "for her own good," which is acceptable, and an abusive exercise of domestic violence, which is not.

Reformist traditionalists usually do not support the practice but search for justifications and alternative interpretations.

This is the text:

> As for those [women] from whom you fear disobedience, admonish them and send them to beds apart and beat them. Then if they obey you, take no further action against them. (4:34)

This Quranic passage offers potential ambiguity in two places: in the term specifying what kind of cause might justify such a response and in the term describing the response itself. Some latch onto the first ambiguity and argue that this passage applies only to very major offenses. While they remain unspecified in the text, Muhammad's contemporaries undoubtedly knew what was meant. They argue that the Arabic term used to describe the wife's offense is closer to "rebellion" than to "disobedience" and suggest that it perhaps was meant to refer to apostasy or to subversive political activity on the part of the wife.

Some authors focus on the second ambiguous term. Traditionalist authorities can spend many paragraphs discussing the exact terminology and concluding that the text does not really mean to "beat" or even to "strike," but should be interpreted as meaning to "lightly tap" (Rauf, 2002). Qaradawi instructs that wives may be hit, but not on the face. The American Muslim publication *Islamic Horizons*, in a special issue dedicated to the topic of domestic violence, proposes in all seriousness that the correct application of this Quranic verse is for the husband to give an errant wife "a few taps" with a "siwak," a kind of toothbrush. This, the author concludes, is "reasonable, dignified, and fairly flawless, for each spouse's human dignity is respected" (Abusulayman, 2003, p. 22). We would be hard-pressed to invent a better illustration for the inability of Islamic traditionalists, even reformist traditionalists, to manage the challenges of modernity than a text like the one above, which earnestly proposes the spectacle of a man resolving disputes by hitting his wife with a toothbrush as an example of a dignified relationship.

For modernists, again, this issue is not a problem. Like the Old Testament, the Quran includes content no longer relevant today, and there is no need to struggle with it. Further, they doubt the authenticity of that sura altogether, since it contradicts what one knows about the Prophet's attitudes and behavior, other passages in the Quran, and the bulk of hadiths concerning marital relations and the appropriate conduct of a husband toward a wife. Numerous hadiths disapprove of marital violence, but these do not make their way to fundamentalist or to conservative traditionalist Web sites. In one such hadith, the Prophet makes the point that it is inappropriate and primitive to hit a person with whom one intends in the future again to be intimate. Famously, the Prophet's final deathbed comment warned men to "fear God in your treatment of women." And finally, due to the intense scrutiny paid to the Prophet's private life by his contemporaries, we have a large number of anecdotes related to disputes he had with his wives. From these stories we know that when he became angry he made sarcastic remarks, sulked, complained to his father-in-law, and at least once withdrew to a different floor of the house for an entire month.

The Quran was not recorded in writing until well after the Prophet's death. It was then assembled by collecting various scraps of bark or bone upon which witnesses to the revelations had recorded them and by locating individuals who had memorized certain suras and having them dictate the text as best they recalled it. This project eventually resulted in the production of several versions of the Quran, which differed from each other. Eventually, to prevent discord, all versions but one were destroyed (see Parwez, 2002). It is widely accepted that at least two suras were lost in that process. Modernists point out that some may also have been falsely or inaccurately recorded. To traditionalists, however, who revere as infallible and divine each letter of the Quran and even the paper it is printed on, that notion is anathema.

Chapter Two

FINDING PARTNERS FOR THE PROMOTION OF DEMOCRATIC ISLAM: OPTIONS

Promoting democracy in the Islamic world and assisting constructively in Islam's process of evolution look to be long-term undertakings. Each of the groups described above presents different challenges and prospects when we examine their potential as partners. "Weighing in" on an ongoing dialogue over values requires us to consider our purpose carefully, to avoid unintended consequences.

THE SECULARISTS

Although there are some ambiguities, Western democracies are premised on the separation of church and state. It follows that the **secularists** should be our most natural allies in the Muslim world.[1]

The problem has been, and continues to be, that many important secularists in the Islamic world are unfriendly or even extremely hostile to us on other grounds. Leftist ideologies, anti-Americanism, aggressive nationalism, and authoritarian structures with only quasi-democratic trappings have been some of the manifestations of Islamic secularism to date.

Another obstacle has been the assumptions Western theorists and policymakers have made that the Islamic world does not accommodate secularism in the same way that other cultures do, seeing that religion as fundamentally political and "this worldly" and that secularism is such a minority position in the Islamic world that it does not make sense to link oneself to its prospects.

This is factually incorrect. Secular regimes have managed to hold power, legitimacy, and even popularity, and secular movements have gained huge follow-

---

[1] And, by the way, that very terminology illustrates the point. We do not speak of the *Buddhist world* or the *Christian world*—and the term *Christendom*, which at times had a geographic dimension, has been archaic for some time. Yet modern international political terminology commonly refers to the *Islamic world* or the *Muslim states*.

ings.[2] One of the Islamic world's most successful states, Turkey, achieved its progress through a policy of aggressive secularism. Turkey also provides a dramatic instance of an Islamic polity transforming itself, in a very short time, from being a deeply Muslim Ottoman state to a laicist system. In this sense, the Turkish case is quite key, perhaps more so than Western policy reflects.

One irony of the post–September 11 situation is that our "hostility threshold" has risen markedly. We are today prepared to accept postures that include a level of hostility to the West, the United States, and Western values, aggressive language and assertive postures that go significantly beyond levels we found unacceptable when they were manifested by nationalists and quasi-socialists in that same part of the world. We can only speculate what different path history might have taken if we had shown some of the socialist Arab nationalists as much indulgence as we are prepared to show some of the fundamentalist extremists today.

There are indications that radical fundamentalism, when it is no longer in an oppositional role but holds power, tends to alienate large segments of the population with the oppressiveness and rigidity of its approach. We should position ourselves to enhance that alienation and utilize the backlash effect. Populations that are exposed to particularly repressive fundamentalism can respond by finding modernism and secularism attractive. By many accounts, this is happening in Iran, especially among students and the young.

In Afghanistan, pious traditional segments of the population, who felt insulted by "foreign" fundamentalists policing and commanding them, and urban middle class and younger segments of the population, who were interested in more freedom and progress, were united in their rejection of Taliban Islam. This backlash encouraged both traditionalism (in the case of older and rural segments) and incipient secularism (in some younger, urban segments).

Fundamentalists and traditionalists commonly allege that secular Western values are the root cause of most social problems, while an Islamic order would ensure morality, strong families, and low crime. Iran is a striking counterargument to these assertions. After decades of strict Islamic governance, Iran is at least as plagued by the problems of the age as any "decadent" Western country. Drug addiction has skyrocketed. Prostitution is a huge problem, so much so that the government seriously contemplated the installation of state-run brothels, officiated over by mullahs,[3] as a way to get some sort of control over

---

[2]See the interesting case Kramer (2001) makes in this regard.

[3]Temporary marriages, allowed in Shi'a Islam, would have been pronounced for the duration of the transaction, lending a note of respectability, as well as providing income to the officiating clergy. The plan unleashed a great deal of controversy. See "Drugs and Prostitution Soar in Iran" (2000), Muir (2000), Muir (2002), and Saba (2000).

the situation. Teenage runaways, alcoholism, escalating crime rates—the imposition of shari'a punishments has not deterred and the vigilant state enforcement of Islamic conduct has not prevented such problems from spiraling out of control.

The example of Iran provides a simple, empirical way to invalidate the claim that the freedom of Western democracy is the problem and that a coercively applied Islam is the answer. The failures of Islamic governance in Iran should be publicized widely, as these facts are not generally known to Islamic audiences, who are thus inclined to believe the simple assertion that shari'a law deters crime and that a more strict application of Islam and Islamic law will solve the problems of society.

THE FUNDAMENTALISTS

We know that the **radical fundamentalists** are hostile to modern democracy, to Western values in general, and to the United States in particular; that their overall goals and visions are incompatible with ours; and that they oppose us and we oppose them. In the past, some experts have felt that it may be possible to work even with the radical fundamentalists in the hopes of engaging and gradually reforming them. In places not central to Western policy—Afghanistan, for example—some even suggested that the usual standards should be suspended and that one should merely attempt to reach a minimal accommodation with those who held power and otherwise turn a blind eye to their conduct.

Post–September 11 thinking has not been hospitable to that view, and such an approach is no longer being seriously proposed as a means of dealing with the current massive threat of fundamentalist extremism. There are two obvious reasons: We have realized that ignoring remote areas makes them suitable as bases for our enemies, and we have realized that views we had thought were marginal and eccentric in fact have more adherents, who are more dangerous than we expected. Thus, accommodation with radical fundamentalists is not currently thought to be a viable choice.

However, as concerns the scriptural fundamentalists, hostilities continue to be suspended and tactical alliances continue in specific cases dictated by tactical or strategic considerations. The obvious example is Saudi Arabia. The possibility of some sort of rapprochement and renegotiated political relationship with Iran remains under consideration.

Clearly, our strategy toward Saudi Arabia is based on geopolitical, tactical, and economic considerations and does not represent an endorsement of that regime or its lifestyle and ideology. However, such tactical alliances have their hazards. They can weaken our credibility and can make us seem lacking in fortitude and principles. For example, as the United States was gearing up to attack the Taliban and al Qaeda in Afghanistan and was accompanying this with a public relations effort to explain why such a backward, oppressive regime needed to be removed from power and prevented from further tyrannizing its people, speeches citing examples of Taliban human rights abuses had to be carefully screened to make sure that the practices one was condemning were not identical to those engaged in by our "friends," the Saudis.[4] Since it is obvious to any observer that this friendship is sustained only by tactical and economic considerations, this clearly weakens our moral authority.

A number of authors believe that fundamentalist hostility to the United States and to the West primarily reflects anger over some aspects of our foreign policy or discomfort over the more-liberal aspects of Western culture. It is important to be aware that, while such concerns play a part, fundamentalism represents a basic and total rejection of democracy and of the core values of modern civil society. It wants, in the words of Algerian Islamic Salvation Front (FIS) spokesperson Ali Benhadj, to "break the neck of democracy" (Kepel, 1998).

The issue is not democracy's imperfect application, its ethnocentrism or excessive pragmatism, or any such flaw, but democracy itself. As stated in the platform of the organization Hizb-ut-Tahrir: "The republican system is based on the democratic system, which is a system of Kufr [unbelief] . . ." (Hizb-ut-Tahrir Web site, undated).

Similarly, *Dangerous Concepts* (Hizb-ut-Tahrir, 1997), a volume widely disseminated in print and on the web by United Kingdom–based Al-Khilafah Publications, lists "nationalism, socialism, democracy, pluralism, human rights, freedom and free-market policies" (p. 6) as the "danger[s] and falla[cies]" (p. 7) by which unbelievers are seeking to "finish off Islam" (p. 7); a later chapter describes terrorism as "a form of prayer" (p. 12).

The above-cited sources can be assigned to the extreme end of the spectrum with relative ease. Such Web sites as IslamOnline present a greater challenge. Whereas the other sources are often characterized by poor English and the use of slogans, the texts on IslamOnline reflect a much higher degree of education and English proficiency, as well as greater sophistication in the presentation of material. For outward reasons alone—because it looks so modern—we might be tempted to consider this a "modernist" discussion forum. In fact, however, this site takes a profoundly antidemocratic stand. The following paragraph, which attacks the efforts to reinterpret Islam in the light of a new historical age,

---

[4]That the Saudis' destruction of historic treasures did not receive as much attention as the Taliban's is also striking. The Saudis systematically annihilated the historic Islamic architecture of the Balkans, which offended their austere Wahhabi aesthetics (Ford, 2001).

also helps explain the centrality of lifestyle issues within the current Islamic debate (Kamal Sultan, 2002):

> The vast majority of those who advocate the historicity of the Qur'an have fully assimilated the Western epistemological and philosophical assumptions. Direct confrontation and military conquest are now secondary tools to dominate cultures and markets. Habits and lifestyles are primary targets of change in order to guarantee an open market based on a free consumer who has an open mind.

Interpretation only has a role when existing Islamic orthodoxy has left a gap of detail and when it becomes necessary to "cross the t's and dot the i's." In illustration, the author cites as legitimate the discussion over whether the Quran, when it instructs believers to wash before prayer and says that they should "wash your feet to the ankles," meant that "the ankles were included" or not. In Western terminology, an "open mind" is a positive thing; in this article, it is the epitome of what should be avoided.

THE TRADITIONALISTS

The traditionalists at first glance have several features that make them seem attractive as potential partners:

- They are a useful counterweight to the fundamentalists, because they enjoy widespread public legitimacy in the eyes of Muslim populations.
- They tend to be more middle-of-the-road, more moderate, a calming influence.
- They are open to, and in fact often proactively seek, interfaith dialogue.
- They do not usually advocate violence, although some of them sympathize with fundamentalists who have chosen that path, to the point of sheltering them, providing them with resources, and abetting their activities.

While fundamentalist groups often consist mostly of young men, traditionalists represent a more normal slice of society: families, older people, women, school children. They are organized; they have institutional structures and leaders and the essential components of public self-presentation: books, speeches, public events, conferences, associations. They are visible and easy to find.

Orthodox Islam contains elements that support democratic, participatory, egalitarian values. These can be filtered out and used to justify reforms.

For all these reasons, it is tempting to choose the traditionalists as the primary agents for fostering democratic Islam, and indeed this appears to be the course that the West is inclined to take. However, some very serious problems argue against making the traditionalists the main agents of modern democratic Islam, as the following subsections will discuss.

Distinguishing Between Traditionalists and Fundamentalists

It is often difficult to distinguish traditionalists from fundamentalists. The difficulty exists on two levels. It is easy to make a mistake and to classify some leader or some group as traditionalist that is in fact a front for more-radical affiliations. But even without a deliberate attempt to mislead, the views and values of the two positions are often so close that only a very fine line divides them. Traditionalists and fundamentalists share views on a large number of subjects, and fundamentalists use the traditionalist infrastructure (mosques, associations, charitable societies, etc.) as cover and as a support system.

There are critical issues on which the traditionalists are closer to the fundamentalists than to any other segment. These issues include shari'a implementation, attitudes toward the West and the United States, gender relations and the status of women, and the nature of the ideal political order, as well as a number of other basic social and judicial issues.

Even the reformist traditionalists, whose views on social and lifestyle issues are more compatible with international modernity, are often much closer to the fundamentalists than to the West on issues of international politics. For example, traditionalists in general widely denounced the September 11 attacks. But this did not translate into blanket condemnation of terrorism and political violence. Sheikh Tantawi, rector of Al Azhar University and a conservative traditionalist, went on record to condemn the killing of civilians and innocent victims in Israel. But he was challenged on this by Yussuf al-Qaradawi, the influential Qatar-based reformist traditionalist, who takes a relatively progressive stance on many social issues but is aggressive on the issue of an "Islamic" foreign policy.[5] He writes (al-Qaradawi, n.d.):

> The Islamic movement should consider itself at the beck and call of every Islamic cause, responding to every cry for help wherever that cry may come from. It should stand with Eritrea in its jihad against the unjust Marxist Christian regime . . . .
>
> It should stand by Sudan against the treacherous Christian racist rebellion . . . .
>
> It should support the Muslims of the Philippines against the biased Christian regime that seeks to annihilate them . . . .
>
> It should help the Muslims of Kashmir in their struggle . . . .
>
> Palestine is the first and foremost Islamic cause . . . for this is a serious stage of the Palestinian cause, a stage where there are plans to . . . realize the old dream

---

[5]Yussuf al-Qaradawi was born in Egypt in 1926 and studied at Al Azhar. His membership in the Muslim Brotherhood brought him several periods of detention in prison. In 1962, Al Azhar sent him to Qatar to organize the country's religious studies system, and he became dean of the law faculty at the University of Qatar. His numerous published books, his active Web site, his NGO (International Association of Islamic Relief), and other activities have made him an influential voice in the current Islamic debate over values. See Hashmi (2002).

of Great Israel that extends from the Nile to the Euphrates and then to the land of Hijaz, Medina and Khaybar.

The overlap between fundamentalists and traditionalists has an important and worrisome infrastructure component. As became increasingly and alarmingly clear in the months following September 11, there is significant blurring between these two groups on the level of mosques, Islamic conferences, and Muslim charitable organizations. Radical fundamentalists are often able to move comfortably within, and to utilize, traditionalist Islamic networks, structures, and support systems.

A basic strain of distrust, resentment, and hostility flavors the attitude of traditionalists toward the modern West and the United States especially. This makes it difficult to distinguish them from the fundamentalists.

For example, consider the paper Muhammad Al-Asi wrote when he was Imam of the Islamic Center in Washington, D.C. (Al-Asi, 2000). "The Western definition of politics," he alleged therein, "is sullied and corrupt, the Islamic definition of politics is clean and healthy." Muslims must "overturn the system of kufr" and avoid "joining the 'modern and developed' world," where "economic exploitation is given a good name under the title of free-market operations and capitalism."

Al-Asi purports to be a traditionalist, but his affiliations and his style of reasoning make that seem questionable. He is a fellow at the Institute of Contemporary Islamic Thought in London, which describes itself as "an intellectual center of the global Islamic movement." The cited paper was written for a conference in Karachi. It challenges Western politics, culture, and economics and shows a disregard for orthodoxy. These are hallmarks of fundamentalism.

When American traditionalists get together for conferences, they often express great alienation and hostility to the West and the United States and usually share the platform with those who articulate fundamentalist views. In September 2002, the organizer of a conference entitled "Islam in America: Rights and Citizenship in a Post 9/11 World," held at the University of California at Berkeley, observed that "fear and oppression" were the main features of the life of Muslims in America, which seems a bit of an overstatement. University of South Florida Professor Sami Al-Arian—who at the time had already been suspended from his teaching position for suspected links to terrorists, for a speech he had given advocating "death to Israel," and for being a close associate of the head of the Palestinian Islamic Jihad—was the conference's featured speaker on "civil rights" (Locke, 2002). In February 2003, he would become one of a group of individuals indicted on terrorism charges.

While only solid intelligence work can uncover the concrete linkages between Islamic organizations and extremist movements, connections between traditionalist platforms and fundamentalist sponsors can often be found even through superficial effort.

For example, traditionalists host a number of Web sites geared to pious Muslims who find themselves in some sort of a lifestyle quandary and want guidance.

One popular site of this kind is ourdialogue.com, consulted by thousands of Muslims worldwide, especially immigrants and migrant workers displaced from their communities and facing unfamiliar issues. Here are some of the worries that prompt people to email their requests for guidance:

1. Can a Muslim be a vegetarian, or does one have to eat meat because the Prophet did?

2. For the ritual washing before prayers, is it necessary for women to unbraid their hair?

3. If you happen upon your husband just as he is writing out the ritual formula to divorce you three times on a piece of paper, with your name clearly cited in the text, but he claims that he was just absentmindedly doodling and did not really mean it, are you divorced or not?

(By the way, the answers are: Yes, you can be a vegetarian; not everything the Prophet did is obligatory for all other Muslims. No, you do not have to unbraid your hair, as long as water touches your scalp. Yes, the divorce counts, but the couple can remarry if they want to.)

Who exactly is issuing these judgments? That question does not seem to be too important to those who seek guidance in this fashion, which in itself is revealing, since it points to a mentality willing to accept authority with few questions. Such Web sites usually do not provide anything like a "bio" listing the names and qualifications of those who review the questions and formulate a reply. The "Our Dialogue" site merely notes that "answers to questions are provided by more than one scholar."

That site is hosted by a Pakistani group, apkar pk, based in Karachi, and many of the questions come from Pakistanis living abroad. But look just a little more carefully, and you learn that the answers come from Saudi Arabia. The Saudi agency "Arab News" sponsors this service for "Muslims in the Subcontinent who cannot get convincing answers from their own nearby Ulama."

A second site, IslamForToday.com, initially makes a very different impression. Glossy, and American in tone, it prominently features progressive, even "uppity" views by Western converts. Its mission statement, right under the logo, is to "improve the image of Islam," and U.S. visitors to the site are clearly the main intended audience. But the positions on key issues are overwhelmingly traditionalist, even fundamentalist.

Tracking this site back by following its list of sponsors and recommended sources, we are sent to the Al Haramein Foundation. But there, of course, the trail ends, because that site will not open, the foundation having been blocked after September 11 as an organization linked to terrorists.[6]

Potentially Useful Democratic Elements

The traditionalist belief set does include democratic elements. It can be made to justify reforms, but not without significant effort. Traditionalists have produced a large number of publications sketching a "kinder, gentler" vision of Islam, in rebuttal of the religion's negative image and of the public statements by radicals, whom they do not wish to be tainted by. These books typically praise the socially positive aspects of Islam, find rationalizations and softened interpretations for practices that are today considered oppressive, and argue that Islam is not only compatible with the principles of the modern age (democracy, equality, social welfare, education) but indeed pioneered them.[7]

Besides their tone, which to various degrees combines defensiveness with apologetics, these writings usually contain positions and philosophies that are fundamentally at odds with modern civil society.

The underlying problem is that the philosophical underpinnings of the two are incompatible. Modern democracy rests on the values of the Enlightenment; traditionalism opposes these values and sees them as a source of corruption and evil. Traditionalism is antithetical to the basic requirements of a modern democratic mind-set: critical thinking, creative problem solving, individual liberty, secularism. One can gloss over these differences for a time, but they will not go away, and sooner or later one will arrive at points of conflict.

Modern democratic civil society will not support shari'a law; traditionalism requires it. Modernity does not go along with the death sentence for adultery or flogging and amputation as acceptable criminal punishments; it will not accommodate enforced gender segregation or extreme and overt discrimination against women in family law, criminal justice, and public and political life. Not all traditionalists seek to implement all these things, but they all defend some of them and are at best ambivalent about the rest.[8] Reformist traditional-

---

[6]The organization has been linked with terrorist groups in a number of countries, including Pakistan, Afghanistan, and Bosnia, as well as Chechnya.

[7]To cite only a few, there are Hofmann (1997), Al-Mamun (1990), Wadud (1999), Ibn Lulu Ibn Al-Naqib (1997), Khalid Arshed (1999), Ali (1992), Kurzman (1998), and Abdessalam (2000).

[8]For example, Qaradawi, in his publication "Issues Concerning Freedom of Belief, the Unity of Islamic Nations and the Backwardness of Some Islamic Nations" takes a liberal position on the practice of other religions and even on apostasy, arguing that as long as a Muslim who renounces his religion does so "without spreading his views among the people and without shaking the

ists do not necessarily want to reinstate all of these practices, but they too accept the underlying principles. Traditionalists by definition believe that the Quran and the shari'a should be followed literally and completely. They can never be negated. At best, they can be circumvented, typically through an elaborate and at times tortured procedure of finding exceptions and clauses and searching out ambiguities and possible alternative interpretations.

Further, traditionalism is causally linked with backwardness and underdevelopment, which in turn are the breeding ground for social and political problems of all sorts. Traditionalism was, throughout much of modern history, the dominant version of Islam, determining the way in which Muslim society was structured. It may look comparatively better today when we contrast it with fundamentalism, but the fact remains that it produced, maintained, and was unable to discover a way out of poverty, backwardness, and underdevelopment.

A major recent study, the United Nations Development Programme's (UNDP's) *Arab Human Development Report*, identified the absence of democracy, the inequitable status of women, and neglect of education as the three key causes of backwardness in the Arab world (UNDP, 2002). Traditionalism is more hierarchical and authority-bound than democratic; is highly leery of women's social and economic integration and participation and places many restrictions on it; and is wary of modern, secular education. The three problems identified in the UNDP report will not be fixed if the traditionalists are in charge—indeed, the traditionalists have presided over societies marked by these persistent problems. And until headway is made on these problems, the region will remain highly unstable and vulnerable to extremist movements.

The Danger of Domestic Backlash

There is the danger of domestic backlash in the West. Islamic traditionalism is highly critical of, and often insulting toward, Western culture. So, it would take considerable forbearance for secular Western publics to seem to accept the criticism that the West is depraved and shallow, that its history has been

---

peoples' belief," he should not be killed, as is the usual penalty. He finds a way around the issue of adultery by theoretically affirming the death penalty—he must do this because he has found it in the hadith—but claiming that the preconditions for that penalty are so stringent as to make the implementation nearly impossible. Not only must there be four witnesses to the actual act of adultery, the guilty parties must also confess. This refers to two somewhat odd hadiths in which the Prophet is related to have been approached voluntarily by adulterers, to have urged them to rescind their confessions, but in the face of their refusal, to have reluctantly been obliged to order their deaths. Qaradawi claims that these are the only two incidents in history when adultery was punished by death. This is a peculiar claim, as it happened repeatedly in Taliban Afghanistan and has been practiced in Iran since the Islamic Republic was instituted. Perhaps he considers these instances to be illegal and hence un-Islamic. On amputation as a punishment for theft, however, Qaradawi holds to the orthodox view. Except in extreme situations—the family is starving—he confirms amputation as a way to avoid theft from becoming a problem in communities due to "excessive leniency."

oppressive, and that it is to blame for many of the problems the rest of the world experiences, while going to great lengths to show admiration for Islam and to accommodate its religiously based demands in a secular world.

In the United States, where the general shock over the September 11 attacks and the ongoing state of emergency, war, and terror preparedness have prompted sustained solidarity and support for a wide range of government measures intended to ensure security, a backlash may be slower in coming.

But in Europe, voters and intellectuals alike are already showing an incipient negative reaction to what they perceive as an excessively naïve embracing of Islamic traditionalism on the part of some Western political leaders.

It used to be the right wing of the European political spectrum that tended to be wary of the alternative values and lifestyle of immigrants, especially Muslim immigrants, and to argue that minorities from very different cultural milieus, if they did not want to assimilate, posed a threat to Western identity and core Western values. As the 2002 elections in France and Holland demonstrated, these worries have already spread to wider segments of the population. In some countries, they are reflected in new legislative policies requiring higher measures of assimilation, such as participation in language classes.

European intellectuals and liberals have also begun to articulate related concerns. In one typical volume, 11 prominent authors, including some noted liberal intellectuals, opinion leaders, and experts on Islam, argued that tolerance was being misapplied (Schwarzer, 2002). Because of fear; ignorance; unwillingness to face facts; concern about strengthening right-wing tendencies and feeding social intolerance; and, in the case of the Germans, a dread of appearing racist, European governments and intellectual leaders had allowed Europe to become the operating base and a safe haven for Muslim extremists and terrorists. Incorrect policies had also inadvertently elevated a backward strain of Islam over its more secular, moderate expression by allowing a small but vocal and aggressive minority of extremists and conservatives to become the self-styled leaders of that community. A deliberate blind eye had been turned to their incendiary activities. They were allowed to run a network of mosques and cultural centers that became autonomous operating cells for terrorists and radicals and to disproportionately influence legislation and public debate.

While U.S. officialdom appears to be seeking a symbolic rapprochement with Islam on the level of outward lifestyle issues, European leaders seem more inclined to try for a rapprochement on political issues they believe to be important to Muslims. The split between the United States and Europe over Iraq is in part attributable to this difference. The United States appears to believe that the "Arab street" will be appeased if the United States seems to accept and honor Islam as a religion and a way of life. Europeans seem more inclined to play to the sector of the Islamic public, both inside Europe and in the Muslim world, that is concerned with foreign policy issues.

The Potential for Weakening Credibility and Moral Persuasiveness

Accommodating traditionalists to an excessive degree can weaken our credibility and moral persuasiveness. An uncritical alliance with traditionalists can be misunderstood as appeasement and fear.

Bernard Lewis (2001) warns that the "anxious, propitiatory posture adopted by (American) spokesmen" leads Muslim audiences to conclude that the United States is in retreat and has gone soft.

Instead, some critics argue, we should be holding firm to our values. "Ecumenicism," when applied unilaterally, risks eroding our own moral position while strengthening that of an unconciliatory opponent. Such gestures are not interpreted as friendship, but as weakness.

That, for example, is precisely the conclusion Shaikh Abdur-Raheem Green (1994) reached when he wrote that

> It is obvious to many Muslims that the West itself does not really believe in "democracy," or indeed any of those ideals, such as "freedom of speech," "human rights" and so on, which it claims to cherish so dearly—except when it suits their self-interest.

Already, some warn, aggressive voices from the Islamic camp are challenging concepts basic to our civilization, such as the universality of human rights. They are declaring them to be a Western invention, not general but culture-specific, and they are seeking to subordinate them to shari'a (Littman, 1999).

> In recent years, representatives of some Muslim states have demanded, and often received, special treatment . . . . As a result, non-diplomatic terms such as "blasphemy" . . . have seeped into the United Nations system, leading to a situation in which non-Muslim governments accept certain rules of conduct in conformity with Islamic law and acquiesce to a self-imposed silence regarding topics touching on Islam . . . . The new rules of conduct being imposed by the Organization of the Islamic Conference (OIC) and acceded to by other states, give those who claim to represent Islam an exceptional status at the United Nations that has no legal basis and no precedent; it therefore gives ample reason for apprehension.

Suspending basic modern values in the hopes of inviting a reciprocal tolerance is a risky approach that may merely embolden the opponent. Given the fact that core values are under attack, it is instead important to affirm the values of Western civilization. (See, for example, Lewis, 1990.)

The Possibility of Undermining Reforms

Accommodation can undermine reform trends. Overendorsing the traditionalists is interference in the ongoing internal reform effort within Islam. De facto, our stance further disadvantages those whose values are genuinely compatible with ours, the modernists.

THE MODERNISTS

The modernist vision matches our own. Of all the groups, this one is most congenial to the values and the spirit of modern democratic society.

Modernism, not traditionalism, is what worked for the West. This included the necessity to depart from, modify, and selectively ignore elements of the original religious doctrine. The Old Testament is not different from the Quran in endorsing conduct and containing a number of rules and values that are literally unthinkable, not to mention illegal, in today's society.[9] This does not pose a problem because few people would today insist that we should all be living in the exact literal manner of the Biblical patriarchs. Instead, we allow our vision of Judaism's or Christianity's true message to dominate over the literal text, which we regard as history and legend. That is exactly the approach that Islamic modernists also propose.[10]

---

[9]See Alan Dershowitz's take on this issue in his debate with Alan Keyes:

> When I burn a bull on the altar as a sacrifice, I know it creates a "pleasing odor for the Lord" (Leviticus 1:9). The problem is my neighbors. They claim the odor is not pleasing to them. How should I deal with this? I would like to sell my daughter into slavery as suggested by Exodus 21:7. What do you think a fair price would be? . . . I have a neighbor who insists on working on the Sabbath. Exodus 35:2 clearly states he should be put to death. Am I obliged morally to kill him myself, or may I hire a hit man? (Dershowitz and Keyes, 2000, p. 5)

A later sentence in this same debate today sounds eerily prescient (p. 7):

> When you give religiously inspired zealots weapons of mass destruction and you promise them that if they kill innocent people they will go to heaven, imagine what the consequences will be.

[10]Khaled Abou El Fadl (2001, p. 94) proposes the following resolution for situations where the literal text conflicts with contemporary values:

> One cannot exclude the possibility that the conviction which has been formulated (concerning the nature and normativities of the Divine) might come into friction with certain determinations of the text. A person can read a text that seems to go against everything that he or she believes about God and will feel a sense of incredulous disbelief, and might even exclaim, "This cannot be from God, the God that I know!" . . .

> It is also possible that an adequate resolution would not be found, and that the individual conscience and the textual determination continue to be pitted in an irresolvable conflict. I argue that . . . in the final analysis, Islamic theology requires that a person abide by the dictates of his or her conscience. A faith-based objection to the determination might be necessary. Faith-based objections are founded on one's sense of iman (conviction and belief in and about God) . . . .

There are other solutions, too. Modernism also applies the principle of *maslaha*, or public good, which goes back to reformist Muslim jurists of the 13th century, as something that was thought to override even the Quran itself.

There are definite indications that change can be effected in Islam. In fact, some explicit and quite major departures from Quranic norms have historically already taken place. Significantly, these did not occur as a result of exhaustive scholarly debate in which one side managed to "out-hadith" the other. Instead, these practices were dropped silently, without any debate at all. The most impressive example is the institution of slavery. The Quran unmistakably and explicitly allows the owning of slaves, but not even the most staunch traditionalist authority would today defend that institution, and radical fundamentalists who cling to the most extreme interpretation of jihad to justify terrorism never make the argument that slavery, since the original Islamic community engaged in it and the Quran permits it, is good and should be reinstituted. Slavery has left Islamic orthodoxy, apparently for good. Yet the issue was never debated on the basis of hadith. An unspoken consensus removed it from orthodoxy. This shows that Islam is no more immune than other major world religions to a changing civilizational consensus on values.

Modernism Has Respected Intellectuals and Leaders

Modernist Islam has many potential leaders and voices, individuals who combine unimpeachable scholarly credentials and thorough knowledge of Islamic doctrine and theology with a modern education and value set. Some are prominent in their local communities or in academic circles. Some "borderline" individuals between modernizing traditionalism and modernism also fit this potential role, such as Mustafa Ceric, the Grand Mufti of Bosnia.

An individual whose writings are better known in the United States is Khaled Abou El Fadl, Professor of Islamic Law at UCLA. A well-regarded modernist scholar and author, his writings criticize the "rampant apologetics" of traditionalists and the "authoritarian, puritanical" approach of the fundamentalists alike. The dire situation of the contemporary Muslim world, he believes, calls for introspection, critical insight, and abandoning the notion that one ought to be involved in a civilizational war with the West.

Muhammad Shahrur, author of the "Proposal for an Islamic Covenant," stresses the need for Arabs to "have a plan to deal with the twenty-first century" that includes political freedom, pluralism, democracy, and equality (Shahrur, 2000). Serif Mardin attempts to bring the concept of civil society into alignment with Islam and Islamic history (Mardin, 1996). Fethullah Gulen puts forward a version of Islamic modernity that is strongly influenced by Sufism and stresses diversity, tolerance, and nonviolence (Gulen, 1999). His writings have inspired a strong multinational following and have proven attractive to young people.[11]

---

[11] Numerous Web sites have been dedicated to his teachings and to making his sayings and articles available; for example, see http://www.mfgulen.com.

Bassam Tibi is an example of a European Muslim modernist. He advocates the deliberate intellectual creation of a reformist Islam, one that is subordinated to the values of modern secular society and international human rights. In the case of diaspora communities, it should additionally incorporate the values and laws of the democratic host country (Tibi, 2002).

Contemporary Iran has produced a number of dissidents who could be put forward as role models, even as inspiring civil rights heroes. Through their public defense of reason and of the right of individuals to make their own moral judgments they have exposed themselves to persecution and become heroes to the Iranian student movement.[12] Their views, experiences, and confrontations with the repressive state authorities should receive much greater publicity.

Weaknesses of the Modernists

On ideological grounds, the modernists are the most credible vehicle for developing and transmitting democratic Islam, but in the current reality, they operate under a number of handicaps that significantly reduce their effectiveness.

Their most basic handicap, which underlies most of the others, is financial. Powerful forces stand behind the fundamentalists and provide them with enormous resources: money, infrastructure, weapons, media and access to other popular platforms, control over educational and welfare institutions, etc.

Traditionalists also have a well-established power base that can include access to significant resources. They collect taxes; receive subsidies and donations; and have independent sources of revenue, such as businesses and foundations. They have a "captive audience" through mosques, schools, and social and welfare programs, supplemented by modern media. Both fundamentalists and traditionalists have their own publishing houses, radio and TV stations, schools, newspapers, etc. Modernists have nothing comparable.

The second handicap is political. Modernists living in a fundamentalist or a traditionalist environment and are politically active are far from having support, and their posture exposes them to danger. They can be accused of apostasy, taken to court, prevented from writing and working, harassed in various ways, and even sentenced to death.[13]

---

[12]The case of Professor Aghajari, sentenced to death by an Iranian court for saying that Muslims were not "monkeys" who should blindly follow the interpretations of senior religious clerics, is particularly noteworthy. His sentence is under review following ongoing major student protests (Iran Expert, 2002).

[13]Egyptian modernist author and medical doctor Nawal as-Saadawi has faced repeated harassment in court on various religious charges. Several Pakistani modernists have been sentenced to death, although the sentences have not been carried out. (Gompu, 1995; Asian Human Rights Commission, 2001; Wiseman, 2002.)

As long as they are operating as isolated individuals, this is a weakness. But in connection with support and a movement, it becomes an asset, in the sense that—like other liberation and civil rights movements—some individuals are prepared to risk jail, to serve as heroes, role models, and leaders.

In the West or in other modern settings, modernists have a different handicap: They tend to be well educated and well integrated. They do not hold sensationalist views that provide interesting sound bites, and they do not proselytize. They tend to write academic texts or editorials, not mass-market propaganda. This makes their work relatively inaccessible to the bulk of the population, especially the restless young. One of the authors cited above, Khaled Abou El-Fadl, writes long, complicated volumes critiquing the different schools and philosophies of Islamic jurisprudence. His analysis of the Saudi religious establishment's more absurd religious fatwas is highly readable and entertaining, but it is buried in an expensive, 361-page-long theoretical volume about the significance and evolution of religious authority in Islam. Bassam Tibi publishes academic books in the field of political science.

Modernists become professors at universities, not teachers in madrassas or at mosque Sunday school. They dress like everyone else, which reduces their attractiveness to journalists who are writing a piece about "Muslims in America," and they do not segregate themselves socially, which makes them harder to find—you cannot just call an Islamic cultural center and find them there. Since Islam is not their overriding personal identity, they are not prone to establishing Islamic organizations or clubs. This gives them poor visibility.

Two Special Cases of Modernism

Two specific variants of modernism need to be considered separately: Islam as practiced by Muslims in the West, and global youth culture.

Western Islam. Millions of Muslims live outside the historic Islamic heartland and have been socialized and educated in the West, where they have either formed their own communities and subculture or assimilated into the dominant society. What influence has this had on their interpretation and practice of Islam? Could they be a resource in developing a modern democratic Islam?

European Islam. In Eastern Europe, Balkan Muslims have developed and now practice an orthodox yet assimilated, secularized, modernist variant of Islam (Schwartz, 2002). Eastern Europe also provides dramatic instances of Western-Islamic friendship and cooperation, such as the (albeit belated) intervention of the West on behalf of persecuted Bosnian and Albanian Muslims. Non-Muslim European civil society rallied impressive support and displayed a high amount of solidarity and initiative. A Catholic organization, Caritas, raised a million dollars in one day just by asking Austrian supermarket shoppers to add a donation to their bill. Interestingly, the campaign played on the notion that the beleaguered Bosnians should be helped because they were "neighbors"—religion was not mentioned.[14] This chapter of recent history deserves more prominence. Hundreds of thousands of Bosnian refugees were warmly taken in by Western European communities and individual families during that conflict.

International criminal courts are applying the principles of secular human rights in an effort to punish those who perpetrated ethnic cleansing against Muslims in the Balkans, seeking justice for them on secular grounds. Balkan Muslims enjoy a higher level of development than most of the Muslim world. This can demonstrate that friendship with the West is possible and that embracing democratic values leads to desirable outcomes and a better quality of life.

At least 9 million Muslims live in Western Europe. The embeddedness of extremist and terrorist organizations within that community has become increasingly and alarmingly known as a consequence of the investigative effort that followed September 11.

However, the data also show that the clear majority of European Muslims is modernist or secularist. One of the intellectual leaders of that community, Bassam Tibi, recommends the active development of "Euro-Islam" as a bulwark against destructive Islamic extremism. This would require gaining better knowledge of what modernist European Muslims believe and how they practice, encouraging this amalgamation of Islam with modernity, and finding ways to codify and disseminate this position, instead of letting traditionalists and fundamentalists—a minority—represent and define European Islam.

European governments have also tended to favor the traditionalist segment, for logistical convenience. France, in particular, has long wanted some sort of an Islamic "church," for the sake of convenience and as a control mechanism. The thought was that the state could then have a single counterpart in its dealings with its Islamic minority. After September 11, the wish to gain a better overview and to create an orthodox, official voice for French Islam increased yet more. This is, however, a strong intervention in the internal power balance of Islam. While the intention was to weaken the extremists, it likewise cut out the modernists and secularists. There is no indication that the ramifications of this move were considered or that alternatives were explored.

American Islam. The same holds true for American Islam. Its "public face" is traditionalist. This is partly by default and partly a consequence of the U.S. government's public diplomacy efforts—a question we will return to later. For now,

---

[14]This project, which ran under the slogan *"Nachbar in Not"* [neighbor in need], was the most successful postwar fund-raising effort ever conducted in Europe. Such instances have not received due coverage.

suffice it to say that letting traditionalism represent American Islam does not reflect sociological reality (Haddad and Lummis, 1987).[15]

European and U.S. studies alike indicate that fundamentalists and traditionalists are in the minority (Smith, 1999).[16] Their ability to speak for Islam and to define its public perception greatly exceeds their numbers and real significance.

One way to correct this image while fostering the development of democracy would be to give greater support to civic and cultural associations arising from within the immigrant and ethnic communities. The artificial over-Islamizing of Western Muslims can be corrected if attention and support are given to the other ways in which they express their identity: music, culture, lectures about history, etc.

The traditionalists have some comparative advantages. They are outspoken and visible. They have an infrastructure of organizations, mosques, and committees. They can draw on external funding. Fundamentalist and traditionalist sources internationally provide them with cheap literature to distribute.

"U.S. mosques, Islamic centers and groceries prominently feature the writings of Maudoodi" (Smith, 1999, p. 46), courtesy of Pakistani fundamentalists, who flood international markets with mass publications of his writings in the form of inexpensive brochures.

Fundamentalists and traditionalists thus currently dominate the discourse. Most books addressed to mass audiences are written by them or reflect their version of Islam. As a small illustration, Maryland public libraries stock a few introductory texts on Islam that are intended to introduce young readers to that

---

[15]Haddad and Lummis focused on immigrants and found that most adapted rapidly to the values and norms of modernity, even when they contradicted the customary beliefs of the place and community of origin.

Another pertinent study distinguished five types of American Muslims (as reported in Kaufman, 2002):

The **liberals** are the most Westernized. Their religious observance concentrates mostly on ceremonial occasions, such as weddings, funerals, and the observation of major holidays.

The **conservatives** are also well integrated. They tend to define the nature of their religious observance for themselves on a family or an individual basis. That observance tends to be somewhat more extensive than that of liberals and includes diet, prayer, and other aspects of personal piety. Their religion is an important, though subsidiary, part of their daily lives.

The **Sufis** follow a more philosophical, mystical interpretation of Islam.

The **evangelicals** seek to visibly orient their entire conduct along Islamic principles. They are less integrated into the broader society, preferring to associate with the like-minded.

The **neonormatives** want to achieve a situation in which everyone lives as observantly as they do and feel that ideally, the entire society or at least their segment of it should be run on strict Islamic principles.

[16]We know that nearly three-fifths of American Muslims are college graduates. Half make more than $50,000 a year, generally in such professions as medicine, management and business, the technology sector, and teaching. Only 20 percent regularly attend mosques.

religion. All of them are written from a conservative traditionalist—verging on a fundamentalist—perspective.

I Am a Muslim (Aggarwal, 1985) is part of a series describing the major religions. It features the 11-year-old son of an extremely conservative and very poor lower-middle-class Pakistani family that recently immigrated to England—not, as we have already noted, an accurate reflection of the relevant demographics. The text asserts as Islamic truth a number of statements that are in fact highly controversial. For example,

> Women are not allowed to pray with men.
>
> A woman should cover herself from the head to the feet except for her hands and face.
>
> Children must obey their parents in all things even when they are grown up.
>
> A girl may be married to someone she has not met before.
>
> In special cases a Muslim man may have more than one wife.

With the exception of the last statement—which is irrelevant for Muslims in England, where polygamy is illegal—none of these statements is correct. Obedience to parents is a value of traditional society, unrelated to Islam. The Quran and the hadith strongly stress the woman's informed consent to marriage, and the Prophet repeatedly offered to dissolve the marriages of girls and women who had not been granted a free choice. Mixed prayer was the norm in the original Islamic community, and Muhammad repeatedly reprimanded men who tried to discourage them from doing so; the debate over this issue remains open today. In this picture book, the female members of Nazir's family, including his three-year-old sister, are completely wrapped in giant shawls. None of the men in the book, though the setting is England, wear Western dress, and most have beards.

The next book on the Montgomery County Library shelf, published in 2002 in the "World of Beliefs" series and lavishly decorated with many illustrations, similarly describes only the fundamentalist and traditionalist versions of the religion. Not one of the dozens of women portrayed in the book is without a head covering, and the majority are heavily veiled. "Muslims believe that women should always be modestly dressed," the text states in major understatement.[17] "In some countries this involves wearing a headscarf, but in others it means being covered from head to foot."

What about the millions of Muslims who do neither? What about the other half of the sura, requiring men to dress modestly as well? In an impressive bit of

---

[17]Already a biased formulation; what the Quran says is that everyone, men and women, should be modestly dressed.

understatement, a picture of three Afghan women in burqas—attractively rendered in watercolors and of multicolored fabric that Taliban religious police would have beaten them for—carries the remark, "These women from Afghanistan are wearing a very conservative style of dress" (Morris, 2002).

Some aspects of U.S. culture also reinforce the traditionalist advantage. Since this is the group most likely to wear Islamic dress, they present a better photo-op, so the media tend to choose them when they need a pictorial illustration for a story about American Muslims. Politicians favor them for the same reason—it is then immediately obvious that they are "reaching out" to Muslims. This approach presents a distorted view of demographic and political realities.

The Department of State's official Muslim Life in America Web site, produced under the auspices of International Information Programs, is exclusively dedicated to traditionalist content,[18] in word and image. The women and girls—even toddlers—wear hijab. A supermarket scene shows two women with even their faces covered. Under the heading "a California family," we see a wife garbed in some self-styled indeterminate dress that has no ethnic or national meaning but looks like it comes from a Bible reenactment. Children participating in a fair, in school sports, and in a youth conference all are shown wearing the most extreme variant of Islamic dress. These pictures do not reflect the mainstream of American Islam but show a marginal segment of the U.S. Islamic community. And the content follows the same approach. There are stories lamenting the fact that the ready assimilation of pupils and students who come to the United States from Islamic countries makes them no longer identifiable as Muslims among their classmates and describing how donning complete hijab, including a floor-length loose dress, makes Muslim high school girls feel like "precious jewels."

This text asserts that "shari'a and its specific provisions are to be scrupulously observed" and speaks of "western influences which may corrupt or subvert basic Islamic values." There is no hint that there might be a range of views on these issues within the U.S. Muslim community. Neither is there any discussion of how the "scrupulous observance of shari'a"—which includes *hudud*, criminal punishments—is going to fit into the U.S judicial system.

Youth Culture, Counterculture. Radical fundamentalism has been very successful in mobilizing youth. The Revolutionary Guards, the Taliban, Hamas, Islamic Jihad, and al Qaeda all have relied on the mass support of the young, especially young men.

---

[18]The URL is http://usinfo.state.gov/products/pubs/muslimlife/. See Appendix B for additional discussion. Note that our observations here were particularly true from the winter of 2001 through the first half of 2002. The Web site has undergone some modifications since then, probably in response to multiple complaints and inquiries from Congress and others, but the basic thrust remains the same.

Fundamentalism has a number of qualities that make it appealing to discontented young people, but it also has important weaknesses that could cause young people to turn against it. This major flaw in fundamentalist political strategy has not so far been exploited.

Fundamentalism's attractiveness to youth is based on the fact that it is provocative and radical and seems to stand for justice and for the downtrodden (especially as symbolized by the Palestinians).

In the Middle Eastern context, Islamic radicalism provides a means of challenging corrupt, foreign-connected, or merely unsuccessful regimes and a way to express one's sentiments on the Palestinian issue. In the West, aggressive Islam is disconcerting to the majority of society, making it an easy and attractive medium for expressing disaffection.

The ideological fuzziness of fundamentalism makes it possible to append any number of individual political agendas and grievances to the message. The program is broad but vague: to end corruption, achieve social justice, obtain a higher moral standard, and make the rest of the world respect Islam. Fundamentalism provides an umbrella for eclectic, effect-driven political radicalism. It offers a quick fix of pride, identity, belonging, and purpose. Membership operates on a shallow, easily acquired level. Most of the instructional materials are tracts rather than books, quickly read. For young people, fundamentalism can function like a sect. Emphasis is on prohibitions, rigid injunctions, and ritual; on the outer form of Islam; and on provocative gestures and signals of intent and solidarity, such as beards and headscarves. The psychological value is obvious: It lends the appearance of structure and discipline, a sense of togetherness and purpose. In more-modern environments, or when the family one wishes to rebel against is more modern or in the West, even something as simple as donning a headscarf is a way to achieve high impact with low effort. It serves as a low-risk "test of courage" and a way to achieve approbation from the "in group." The annoyance and confusion it generates in the secular or more-modern environment gives instant gratification.

However, radical fundamentalism has many features that should turn young people against it. Their support of it is counterlogical, since it is against their objective interests on important counts.

It does not value their lives very highly. By appealing to youthful idealism, and to their sense of drama and heroics, radical Islam turns young people into cannon fodder and suicide bombers. Madrassas specifically educate boys to die young, to become martyrs. If Muslim youth ever begin to look at things through a generational lens, as Western youth did in the 1960s, they may begin to ask why most suicide bombers and martyrs are under the age of 30. You don't have to be young to strap explosives on yourself. If it's such a wonderful thing to do, why aren't more adults doing it?

Fundamentalism operates against the natural impulses and the biology of youth and adolescence. Romantic and sexual impulses are a normal part of that age group. Fundamentalism demands that these be suppressed or rigorously sublimated. It thus violates a significant number of the psychological needs, as well as the economic and other objective interests of young people.

Fundamentalism is playing a demographically very risky game. So far, it has managed to conceal from the vast majority of the population—women and the young—that they are being dominated to their detriment by a small minority.

The demographics of Arab and Muslim societies are hugely weighted toward youth. Fundamentalism has managed to get a demographically powerful younger generation to let itself be manipulated and dominated by a minority of authoritarian older men. If the young people came to realize this, a backlash youth movement could result.

Fundamentalist Islam is inimical to women, half the population. As with youth, the ideology has thus far managed to either incapacitate women as political actors or to delude them into supporting conditions that oppose their objective best interest.

Traditionalism, which is a low-key, moderate ideology associated with what one's parents and grandparents stand for, is at a disadvantage relative to fundamentalism as a way of inspiring youth. Modernism, on the other hand, being bolder and more unconventional, could be a competitor. It also has the advantage of being in the objective better interest of young people and women.

Sufis

Sufis are not a ready match for any of the categories, but we will here include them in modernism. Sufism represents an open, intellectual interpretation of Islam. Sufi influence over school curricula, norms, and cultural life should be strongly encouraged in countries that have a Sufi tradition, such as Afghanistan or Iraq. Through its poetry, music, and philosophy, Sufism has a strong bridge role outside of religious affiliations.

Chapter Three

A PROPOSED STRATEGY

The problem of Islamic radicalism—its manifestations, its underlying causes, and its propensity to meld with other social and political conflicts—makes this an extremely complex issue. There is no one correct approach or response, and there certainly is not one identifiable "fix." Instead, what is called for is a mixed approach that rests on firm and decisive commitment to our own fundamental values and understands that tactical and interest-driven cooperation is simply not possible with some of the actors and positions along the spectrum of political Islam but that possesses a sequence of flexible postures suitable to different contexts, populations, and countries.

This approach seeks to strengthen and foster the development of civil, democratic Islam and of modernization and development. It provides the necessary flexibility to deal with different settings appropriately, and it reduces the danger of unintended negative effects. The following outline describes what such a strategy might look like:

- Support the modernists first, enhancing their vision of Islam over that of the traditionalists by providing them with a broad platform to articulate and disseminate their views. They, not the traditionalists, should be cultivated and publicly presented as the face of contemporary Islam.

- Support the secularists on a case-by-case basis.

- Encourage secular civic and cultural institutions and programs.

- Back the traditionalists enough to keep them viable against the fundamentalists (if and wherever those are our choices) and to prevent a closer alliance between these two groups. Within the traditionalists, we should selectively encourage those who are the relatively better match for modern civil society. For example, some Islamic law schools are far more amenable to our view of justice and human rights than are others.

- Finally, oppose the fundamentalists energetically by striking at vulnerabilities in their Islamic and ideological postures, exposing things that neither the youthful idealists in their target audience nor the pious traditionalists can approve of: their corruption, their brutality, their ignorance, the bias and manifest errors in their application of Islam, and their inability to lead and govern.

Some additional, more-direct activities will be necessary to support this overall approach, such as the following:

- Help break the fundamentalist and traditionalist monopoly on defining, explaining, and interpreting Islam.

- Identify appropriate modernist scholars to manage a Web site that answers questions related to daily conduct and offers modernist Islamic legal opinions.

- Encourage modernist scholars to write textbooks and develop curricula.

- Publish introductory books at subsidized rates to make them as available as the tractates of fundamentalist authors.

- Use popular regional media, such as radio, to introduce the thoughts and practices of modernist Muslims to broaden the international view of what Islam means and can mean.

THE HADITH WARS

Much of the current effort to reform Islam centers on debates over specific rules and practices in orthodox Islam that outsiders to that religion criticize and that no longer seem in step with the current age. The Quran, as the holy book, is generally (though not universally) considered to be beyond critique. However, there are many topics that it does not cover at all or to which it refers only ambiguously. Almost since the inception of Islam, proponents of opposing views have put their own visions and interpretations forward on the basis, primarily, of hadith. We can refer to this form of ideological conflict as the "hadith wars."

The values of civil society and democracy can be defended on the grounds of hadith, and this was the approach we originally investigated during the research phase of this report. However, in the end, hadith can never be more than a secondary, tactical tool, for a number of reasons. In any case, hadith does not provide a way to decide an issue. It always allows room for diametrically opposed views to claim equal legitimacy.

Some argue that one should not engage with fundamentalists and traditionalists on the level of hadith. For example, Ibn Warraq (1995, p. 293) believes that

> to do battle with the orthodox, the fanatics, and the mullahs in the interpretation of these texts is to do battle on their terms, on their ground. Every text that you produce they will adduce a dozen others contradicting yours. The reformists cannot win on these terms—whatever mental gymnastics they perform . . . [1]

However, while the hadith wars can perhaps not be won, they can conceivably be lost or at least forfeited, which—at a time when such a large proportion of the Muslim population is illiterate, uneducated, submissive to local authorities,

---

[1] However, in my interview with him, Mr. Warraq conceded that a frontal critique of Islam was not realistic at this time, and that efforts to promote a kinder, gentler, "defanged" Islam were likely to achieve better results. (Warraq interview, February 22, 2002, via email.)

and bound by tradition—would be unwise. Progressive elements that are obliged to operate in Islamic settings need enough ammunition to achieve at least a stalemate. It is not desirable for fundamentalist Islam to become the default version.

In theory, the study of hadith is a science and, indeed, a highly complex one. But in practice, the rigorous standards are meaningless, and politics reign supreme.

Hadith is supposed to be judged by multiple complicated variables, the first of which is the context and reliability of the hadith:

- Who is the original source?
- How long was he or she a Muslim?
- How close was he or she to the Prophet?
- How directly involved was he or she in the event that is being narrated?
- Is there any independent corroboration?
- Which other narrations stem from this person?
- How reliable are *they* judged to be?
- How intelligent and educated was the person?
- Did the person remember the event or rely on notes?
- Did the person have a vested interest or were they a neutral observer?
- How was this narration passed along?
- Are there gaps in the transmission?
- How reliable are the transmitters?

A separate chain of analysis deals with the substance of the narration:

- Is it a saying of the Prophet that is being reported, or an action he performed, or both?
- If he did a particular thing, one can deduce that this thing is allowed?
- If something was done in his presence by others, and he refrained from reprimanding them, is it likewise allowed?
- What was the context? For example, might he have been joking?

Finally, there are considerations of principle that allow hadith to be placed in a hierarchy:

- Does the application of a particular hadith benefit the common good, or just the interests of an individual?

- Does it make community life easier or harder?
- Do jurists and community practice agree on the issue, or are they at odds?

When scholars list just "some of the rules" that apply to the evaluation and application of hadith, they need seven densely written pages.[2]

But in practice, no such effort is made to weigh and assess, to consider the circumstances and origins of a hadith or the credibility of its narrator. In reality, hadith operates on the level of folk sayings, gaining credibility and popularity through repetition and pithiness. The Islamic Web sites referred to earlier frequently mention hadith, but very rarely do they bother even to cite a source or to say which collection they have drawn a particular hadith from or which version they used. They simply "allege" a hadith.

Even if that were not the case, objectively speaking, there is little doubt that hadith is at best a dubious, flawed instrument. Consider that Al-Bukhari is the compiler of what is generally considered to be the most authoritative and reliable collections of hadith. He collected 600,000 hadith, examined them for their authenticity, eliminated all but 7,600 of them, deleted some for redundancy, and was left with a collection of about 4,000. Mabrook Ismaeel (2003) remarks,

> Let us look at the parameters of Al Bukhari's claim. If we allow one single hour to process each hadith he would have had to work non-stop for about seventy years. Each hadith would have had to be traced back to the Prophet through a long transmission chain each link of which had to be closely examined, with each chain consisting of six or seven individuals of successive generations, all but one of whom were dead. Yet he is said to have completed this work in sixteen years. Was it physically possible for Al-Bukhari to have examined that many hadith? The answer is no.

What hadith cannot do is to decide any issue substantively and authoritatively. Essentially, the "hadith wars" are wars of attrition. The issues that can be debated are endless, branching out into ever more minutiae. The process is, to borrow a term from another religion, Talmudic. This is not the road to change. The excellence of the argument on any particular issue does not persuade people to change their worldview; rather, their worldview determines which expert they consult, which interpretation they will lean toward, which hadith they will pluck out of the vast store.

---

[2]These rules include such things as the following: A saying corroborated by a deed outweighs a mere saying. A text that signifies both a rule and the occasioning factor behind it outweighs a text with only a rule. An explicit saying of the Prophet outweighs a deed of the Prophet. A positive command (do such-and-such) outweighs a negative command (do not do such-and-such). An analogy involving an operative cause that has been ascertained through the method of elimination of alternatives outweighs an analogy involving an operative cause that has been ascertained through the test of suitability. El Fadl (2001), p. 40 ff.

For example, fundamentalists might say that music is forbidden. When the Taliban took power in Afghanistan, they immediately banned all music with the exception of religious recitation. But we have evidence that the Prophet liked secular music. On one occasion, he reproached his wife for forgetting to hire singers for a wedding she was organizing. He then sang for her a stanza of the traditional wedding song he thought ought to have been performed during that event. On another occasion, when a troop of entertainers was passing through, he not only allowed them to perform, he even let them use his mosque as the venue. And he brought his wife Aisha to see them. From those two small incidents, more liberal-minded scholars derive multiple conclusions: Singing is acceptable, indeed it must be a good thing, if the Prophet himself personally engaged in it. And secular singing is OK—this was a wedding song, nothing religious. It is all right for popular entertainment to be enjoyed by a mixed audience—the Prophet encouraged his own wife to attend a performance with him. Lighthearted entertainment has value, otherwise the Prophet would not have permitted it in the mosque.

But that does not mean the issue is closed. What about women singing on television—does the hadith extend so far as to allow that, too? The Supreme Justice of Afghanistan thinks not and has banned it. What if the lyrics, while harmless, are totally nonsensical, therefore untrue? The Quran says that if something is not a truth, then it is an error. Does that not mean the song is spreading error? Or does it depend on the intent, so that if you are listening to music to relax virtuously, it is permissible, but if you are listening to put yourself into a party mood during which you then might feel like going to a night club and drinking, it is bad? Obviously, we now need to discuss the issue of intentions, which is the subject of several Quranic passages and many, many hadiths and subsequent interpretations.[3] The debate over music alone can extend into infinity.

Let us consider a graver issue, the question of whether an Islamic government should police and punish departures from the religious code. Liberals say no: Faith is a matter of individual conscience; each person is accountable only to God, who can know their true intentions, and it is actually an act of un-Islamic impiety to think that you can spy on, judge, and punish your fellow Muslims.

Liberals have hadiths to back that up:

> Remind the people, for you are nothing but a reminder to them. You do not control them. (Quran 88:21)

> Will you then compel mankind, against their will, to believe? (Quran 99)

---

[3]These are only a few of the considerations reviewed by al-Qaradawi when he formulated his own reformist traditionalist position on singing. See "The Forbidden and the Allowed in Islam (at http://www.qaradawi.net; note that the site is in Arabic).

> Let there be no compulsion in religion. (Quran 256)

> He who seeks out the faults of his fellows will have his own faults sought out by Allah, and he whose faults are sought out by Allah will be exposed by Him, even though he may hide in the interior of his house. (al-Tirmidhi)

> Abu Huraira reported that Allah's Messenger said, "Avoid suspiciousness, for suspiciousness is a grave error. And do not be distrustful about one another and do not spy upon one another, and do not feel envy towards each other, and nurse no malice, and entertain no aversion or hostility towards one another. But be like members of a family and servants of Allah." (Muslim)

But supporters of a religious police have their own set of hadiths and suras:

> We sent all these prophets, bringing good news and delivering warnings, so that men might have no further excuse before Allah. (Quran 4:165)

> Let there be of you a community who enforce the things which are commanded and interdict the things which are forbidden; and it is they, they who are effective. (Quran 3:104)

> You must decidedly see that the commanded things are done, and the forbidden things are prevented, or else Allah in due time will visit you with penalties, and you will call on him but he will no longer answer your call. (al-Tirmidhi)[4]

Hadith is susceptible to misuse. Islam is not necessarily a very "accessible" religion. The Quran is difficult to read, even if we disregard the fact that huge segments of the Muslim population cannot read it because they are illiterate, or cannot understand it because they do not understand Arabic. There are translations, but many Muslims feel the text is only valid in the original revelation.

Of additional great importance are the legal opinions that say how Quranic injunctions should be interpreted and applied. There are four orthodox Sunni schools of law that determine this (plus the Shi'a Jaafari school). Although their rulings vary—differing, for example, over whether and under what circumstances you can remarry someone from whom you have been divorced or when thieves should have their hands amputated—they are considered equally correct. Countries or at least regions usually are affiliated with one or the other school of law, but the study is arcane and the application complicated.

Many fascinating examples of how hadith translates into social policy can be found in Khaled Abou El Fadl's authoritative study, *Speaking in God's Name* (El Fadl, 2001). He reviews the often fantastic leaps of logic that have enabled ultra-conservative Saudi jurists to issue religious decisions or fatwas on such topics as high heels, the Wonderbra, and air travel by women. Fatwas can manipulate theological content in a variety of ways. The scholar can draw on a hadith with-

---

[4]Assembled by Muhammad Al-Asi (2000).

out mentioning the fact that most scholars consider that particular hadith shaky. He can take a hadith out of context. Or he can draw questionable analogies to apply ancient hadiths to contemporary issues. Obviously, there are no existing hadiths for many of the troubling issues that come up day to day in the third millennium. In deciding which general principle to apply, the scholar has great leeway, especially if he is part of a movement such as Wahhabism, where other scholars share his worldview and will back his interpretation.

To cite only one example, the Saudi religious institute was consulted by a woman whose habit it had been to visit the grave of her deceased husband but who had now been warned by some neighbors that pious women should not be visiting cemeteries. The Saudi jurists studied the matter and forbade her any further visits. Their reason, however, was not that they had found in the Quran or in the religious tradition any direct mention of such a prohibition. Rather, their reasoning was that her example might inspire other women to also begin visiting the cemetery to pray for departed loved ones. Next thing you knew, cemeteries would become infamous as places where females congregated, which would draw men who wanted to ogle and possibly molest these women, which would lead to immorality. Immorality was un-Islamic, therefore, so was the visiting of their relatives' graves by women.

The effort to foster democratic Islam requires three parallel lines of action in relation to hadith and its impact on the law.

The public in general should be better informed and educated about the process of interpreting their religion, so as not to be at the mercy of unscrupulous or uneducated self-appointed authorities. Rather than accepting that, if some statement claims to base itself on a hadith, they need to understand the complexity of what hadith really means and how interpretations are supposed to be developed. There are innumerable Islamic scholars who can easily explain this, but they are not the ones who are running the religious education programs—formal and informal, legal and illegal—in the Islamic world. They need to make an effort to raise the standard of religious knowledge, to turn Muslims into "educated consumers" of hadith and fatwas and interpretations.

At the same time, until that can be accomplished, a body of "counterhadith" should be made available to those who want more-tolerant, egalitarian, democratic societies but are being persuaded that the changes they seek are "un-Islamic." It is quite easy to assemble the necessary evidence that will support reform and liberalism. There are not that many contentious topics. They could be covered by half a dozen handbooks or pamphlets.

Finally, in recent years, some movement has occurred in the areas of Islamic law, Islamic constitutions, and the like. The more interesting work of Muslim jurists has occurred where they took an eclectic approach, not restricting themselves to just one of the law schools but blending Islamic laws and interpretations from a variety of countries and sources with civil law, international norms, and new looks at orthodox Islamic concepts. This work has taken place in scattered locations. It should be centrally collected and made available to jurists and other interested audiences across the Islamic world.

HIJAB AS A CASE STUDY

The current Islamic debate is so contentious that smaller issues easily become freighted with vast ideological and symbolic significance. Non-Muslim political actors can easily misjudge the significance of an issue and end up endorsing a position that they think "does not matter," without sufficiently realizing its actual ramifications.

For example, showing active approval of the wearing of hijab by Muslim women in the United States can be intended, on the part of U.S. opinion leaders, to convey the message that Muslims are completely free to practice their faith in the United States; that members of other religions can dress differently from the mainstream yet still be accepted; that the United States is a society tolerant of diversity. However, a Muslim woman's head covering is not analogous to the Sikh turban or the Jewish man's yarmulke or even to a sari or other kind of ethnic dress. Unlike hijab, these garments are not the subject of bitterly contentious debates within their communities, and people are nowhere being forced to wear them on pain of beatings, mutilation by acid, or even death. One can cast "hijab" as an issue of freedom of expression and of pluralism, but that ignores the larger context. And the larger context is that "hijab" is neither a neutral lifestyle issue nor a religious requirement. It has become a political statement.[1]

Throughout the Islamic world, the debate over what Islam does and does not require in terms of women's dress and their freedom to participate in society is under intense debate. Governments have taken various positions on the issue, allowing, forbidding, or requiring Islamic dress and headscarves in public

---

[1]In Afghanistan, women who have removed the burqa report being threatened with death, and there have been several incidents of acid being thrown on women who were not wearing it. In Iran, the slogan of enforcers was "cover your head or be beaten on the head." Saudi Arabia's Wahhabi establishment has even forced hijab on U.S. servicewomen stationed there, a situation which is currently the subject of a lawsuit against the military. ("Female Fighter Pilot Sues Over Required Muslim Dress," 2001.)

schools by law. Each of these stances has caused protests, demonstrations, law-suits, and even riots.

Refusing to engage on this topic in an attempt to avoid its becoming a bigger issue *might* be a clever way to take the wind out of the sails of the fundamental-ists and traditionalists.[2] But equally, it might strengthen them and harm the modernist forces. In the U.S. context, wearing hijab is "seen as winning a battle against American culture" (Hasan, 2002, p. 37).

In the United States, hijab is typically worn by the following groups: recent immigrants from rural, traditional parts of the Muslim world; fundamentalists; unassimilated traditionalists belonging to the strongly observant minority; the elderly; and young women who want to get attention and make a provocative statement in their schools, colleges, or workplaces. Even added together, they amount only to a small fraction of U.S. Muslims. Even among new immigrants, only a minority supports hijab.[3]

In the United States, hijab is becoming politicized in some troubling ways. U.S. Muslim women who attend any sort of Islamic events, or who come into con-tact with Muslim student groups, complain about being aggressively con-fronted by traditionalists and fundamentalists who lecture them about not dressing properly. Hijab is associated with female subordination. Among fun-damentalist and traditionalist men, "having a wife who wears hijab, stays home and doesn't question his decisions is a status symbol." At Islamic conferences in the United States, "women not wearing the scarf are booed when they try to speak" (Hasan, 2002).

In short, far from being a placid "lifestyle" issue suitable for demonstrating the U.S. propensity toward pluralism and tolerance, hijab is a minefield. Concerned American Muslims describe the hijab question as being "out of control," as having become an oppressive "litmus test for a woman's Islamic credentials," as exposing women to job discrimination and harassment by making them the most overtly visible symbols of Muslim nonassimilation, and as "exacerbating the problems of American Muslims, not solving them" (Marquand, 1996).

The U.S. mainstream seems unaware of these complexities. A typical article in the *Washington Post* reviewed hijab uncritically, almost gushingly, as a "meaningful expression of identity," something that requires the wearer to

---

[2]This has worked, for example, in Austria, where the government's policy of allowing scarves in public schools has resulted in those scarves being a nonissue, and of gradually decreasing. How-ever, the Muslim minority in Austria is different from the one in France or in Germany, and the political groupings that want to politicize the matter are not present. One approach does not work universally.

[3]In the survey in Haddad and Lummis (1987), less than half of immigrant Muslims thought hijab was a requirement of Islam.

"build herself intellectually." A University of Maryland professor ventured the judgment that the scarf was a "healthy way for the women to express their feelings and blend their American culture with Muslim pride" (Wax, 2002).[4] There was no mention in the article of a contrary or dissenting view, no hint that many Muslim women oppose and resent hijab and that its religious validity is the subject of a major ongoing dispute, and no effort to evaluate the trend sociologically.

The flavor of the debate is different in Europe. Liberal intellectuals there warn that the headscarf

> symbolizes the militant intentions of holy warriors. You can recognize the Islamists and their naïve supporters by this issue. Consider the case of Fereshta Ludin, who wanted to wear her "little personal scarf" as a teacher in the German public school system. From the *taz* to the Süddeutsche Zeitung and even *Die Zeit*, her defeat in court over this issue was greeted by a wave of dismay. But who was this Fereshta Ludin? An Afghan married to a German convert, educated in Saudi Arabia, she and her husband were frequent guests of the Taliban. Ever since 1979, when Iranian women were punished by the Revolutionary Guards if their headcovering slipped out of place, it should have been obvious that this headcovering was not a "religious custom" or a "little personal matter" but a highly political issue, that indeed the scarf serves as the flag of the Islamic crusade.[5]

It is correct that the hijab issue mirrors the broader debate. The fundamentalists determined its signal value—just as a junta takes over the radio station as its first symbolic act, fundamentalists signal their advances by immediately imposing the head covering on women wherever they gain in strength and influence.

In spring 2003, the U.S. State Department Web site "Muslim Life in America" contained 32 images of women and girls and even female toddlers below the age that veiling would be considered appropriate in strict Islamic countries, wearing hijab. By contrast, it contains only 13 pictures of women and girls with their heads not covered. This is a serious visual misrepresentation of how the U.S. Muslim community lives, and an apparent U.S. government endorsement of hijab.[6]

---

[4]It is also noteworthy that the article appears in the Metro section, not on the religion page.

[5]*Taz* is a nickname for the *Tages Anzeiger* newspaper.

[6]This was particularly true in the winter of 2001 through the first half of 2002. The Web site has undergone some modifications since then, probably in response to multiple complaints and inquiries from Congress (one example is reproduced in this report as Appendix D) and others, but the basic thrust remains the same.

STRATEGY IN DEPTH

The following describes, in somewhat more detail, how the recommendations in Chapter Three could be implemented.

BASIC POINTS OF THE STRATEGY

Build Up a Modernist Leadership

Create role models and leaders. Modernists who risk persecution should be built up as courageous civil rights leaders, which indeed they are. There are precedents showing that this can work. Nawal Al-Sadaawi achieved international renown for enduring persecution, harassment, and attempts to prosecute her in court on account of her principled modernist stand on issues related to freedom of speech, public health, and the status of women in Egypt. Afghan interim minister of women's affairs Sima Samar inspired many with her outspoken stance on human rights, women's rights, civil law, and democracy, for which she faced death threats by fundamentalists. There are many others throughout the Islamic world whose leadership can similarly be featured.

Include modern, mainstream Muslims in political "outreach" events, to reflect demographic reality. Avoid artificially "over-Islamizing the Muslims"; instead, accustom them to the idea that Islam can be just one part of their identity.[1]

Support civil society in the Islamic world. This is particularly important in situations of crisis, refugee situations, and postconflict situations, in which a democratic leadership can emerge and gain practical experience through local NGOs and other civic associations. On the rural and neighborhood levels, as well, civic associations are an infrastructure that can lead to political education and a moderate, modernist leadership.

---

[1] This idea is more extensively developed in Al-Azmah (1993). Al-Azmah is himself a "Euro-Muslim."

Develop Western Islam: German Islam, U.S. Islam, etc. This requires gaining a better understanding of the composition, as well as the evolving practice and thought, in these communities. Assist in eliciting, expressing, and "codifying" their views.

Go on the Offensive Against Fundamentalists

Delegitimize individuals and positions associated with extremist Islam. Make public the immoral and hypocritical deeds and statements of self-styled fundamentalist authorities. Allegations of Western immorality and shallowness are a cherished part of the fundamentalist arsenal, but they are themselves highly vulnerable on these fronts.

Encourage Arab journalists in popular media to do investigative reporting on the lives and personal habits and corruption of fundamentalist leaders. Publicize incidents that highlight their brutality—such as the recent deaths of Saudi schoolgirls in a fire when religious police physically prevented Saudi firefighters from evacuating the girls from their burning school building because they were not veiled—and their hypocrisy, illustrated by the Saudi religious establishment, which forbids migrant workers from receiving photographs of their newborn children on the grounds that Islam forbids human images, while their own offices are decorated by huge portraits of King Faisal, etc. The role of "charitable organizations" in financing terror and extremism has begun to be more clearly understood since September 11 but also deserves ongoing and public investigation.

Assertively Promote the Values of Western Democratic Modernity

Create and propagate a model for prosperous, moderate Islam by identifying and actively aiding countries or regions or groups with the appropriate views. Publicize their successes. For example, the 1999 Beirut Declaration for Justice and the National Action Charter of Bahrain broke new ground in the application of Islamic law and should be made more widely known.

Criticize the flaws of traditionalism. Show the causal relationship between traditionalism and underdevelopment, as well as the causal relationship between modernity, democracy, progress, and prosperity. Do fundamentalism and traditionalism offer Islamic society a healthy, prosperous future? Are they successfully meeting the challenges of the day? Do they compare well with other social orders? The UNDP social development report (UNDP, 2002) points clearly to the linkage between a stagnant social order, oppression of women, poor educational quality, and backwardness. This message should be energetically taken to Muslim populations.

Build up the stature of Sufism. Encourage countries with strong Sufi traditions to focus on that part of their history and to include it in their school curricula. Pay more attention to Sufi Islam.

Focus on Education and Youth

Committed adult adherents of radical Islamic movements are unlikely to be easily influenced into changing their views. The next generation, however, can conceivably be influenced if the message of democratic Islam can be inserted into school curricula and public media in the pertinent countries. Radical fundamentalists have established massive efforts to gain influence over education and are unlikely to give up established footholds without a struggle. An equally energetic effort will be required to wrest this terrain from them.

SPECIFIC ACTIVITIES TO SUPPORT THE STRATEGY

Thus, to accomplish the overall strategy, it will be necessary to

- Support the modernists and mainstream secularists first, by
  - publishing and distribute their works
  - encouraging them to write for mass audiences and youth
  - introducing their views into the curriculum of Islamic education
  - giving them a public platform
  - making their opinions and judgments on fundamental questions of religious interpretation available to a mass audience, in competition with those of the fundamentalists and traditionalists, who already have Web sites, publishing houses, schools, institutes, and many other vehicles for disseminating their views
  - positioning modernism as a "counterculture" option for disaffected Islamic youth
  - facilitating and encouraging awareness of pre- and non-Islamic history and culture, in the media and in the curricula of relevant countries
  - encouraging and supporting secular civic and cultural institutions and programs.
- Support the traditionalists against the fundamentalists, by
  - publicizing traditionalist criticism of fundamentalist violence and extremism and encouraging disagreements between traditionalists and fundamentalists
  - preventing alliances between traditionalists and fundamentalists

- — encouraging cooperation between modernists and traditionalists who are closer to that end of the spectrum, increase the presence and profile of modernists in traditionalist institutions

- — discriminating between different sectors of traditionalism

- — encouraging those with a greater affinity to modernism—such as the Hanafi law school as opposed to others to issue religious opinions that, by becoming popularized, can weaken the authority of backward Wahhabi religious rulings

- — encouraging the popularity and acceptance of Sufism.

- Confront and oppose the fundamentalists, by

  - — challenging and exposing the inaccuracies in their views on questions of Islamic interpretation

  - — exposing their relationships with illegal groups and activities

  - — publicizing the consequences of their violent acts

  - — demonstrating their inability to rule to the benefit and positive development of their communities

  - — targeting these messages especially to young people, to pious traditionalist populations, to Muslim minorities in the West, and to women

  - — avoiding showing respect or admiration for the violent feats of fundamentalist extremists and terrorists, instead casting them as disturbed and cowardly rather than evil heroes

  - — encouraging journalists to investigate issues of corruption, hypocrisy, and immorality in fundamentalist and terrorist circles.

- Selectively support secularists, by

  - — encouraging recognition of fundamentalism as a shared enemy, discouraging secularist alliances with anti-U.S. forces on such grounds as nationalism and leftist ideology

  - — supporting the idea that religion and the state can be separate in Islam, too, and that this does not endanger the faith.

CORRESPONDENCE ABOUT THE U.S. DEPARTMENT OF STATE'S PORTRAYAL OF ISLAM

Congressman Tom Lantos (D-Calif.) sent the following letter to Secretary of State Colin Powell in 2002.[1]

Mr. Secretary,

As you know, I have long taken a special interest in America's public diplomacy, which I view as a vital element of our overall foreign policy. Battling for "hearts and minds" around the world—providing the educational tools, informational programs, and human exchanges that give people the opportunity to judge for themselves the logic of our policies and the attraction of our values—is an essential component of the "war on terrorism." I am delighted that, under your leadership, this long-neglected aspect of U.S. diplomatic engagement has received heightened attention.

In this context, I write to express my disappointment and dismay with some of the Public Diplomacy material I have seen produced by the State Department and transmitted abroad. I would especially draw your attention to the following:

- The State Department's widely disseminated booklet "Network of Terrorism." This handsome, glossy brochure is designed to make the case for the U.S.-led international campaign against terrorism by laying out the factual material in a dispassionate, lawyerly fashion. In doing so, it highlights condemnations of the September 11 attacks by prominent Muslim clerics. This is a fine idea, but I do not understand why the Department chooses to honor in an official publication clerics who have otherwise sanctioned suicide bombings (like Yusuf al-Qaradawi) or have uttered some of the most vile anti-Semitic epithets (like Abdul Rahman Sudais)? In the war on terrorism, these people are our adversaries, not our friends, regardless of what they may or may not have said about September 11. And in the larger fight for "hearts and minds," lending any imprimatur to any of their views is misguided, as well as misleading of U.S. policy and values.

- The State Department's "Islam in the U.S.—Overview: Background Materials" website (http://usinfo.state.gov/usa/islam/overview.htm). Evidently, this

---

[1]Transcript provided to the author by congressional staff member Alan Makovsky in an email dated September 30, 2002. Reproduced with permission.

website is designed to provide a one-stop research guide to Islam and American Muslim life. I seriously question, however, the appropriateness of some of the material presented on this website. In particular, the website features an e-book published by The Middle East Institute called Introduction to Islam. I cannot understand why the U.S. government would promote such a work. Do we promote equivalent books for Christianity, Judaism, Hinduism, or Buddhism? We do not, and we should not. And Islam should be treated no differently than other American religions. Interpretation of religions is the purview of scholars and practitioners of religion. Whatever the views of given U.S. officials, the U.S. government institutionally should not be seen as promoting one interpretation, as embodied in one book. Separately, given the prohibition on public diplomacy activities targeting domestic audiences, whom exactly do we intend to influence with this publication? Presumably, the Islamic world audiences for which this website seems intended do not need an introduction to Islam. And I doubt other foreign audiences will seek background information on Islam from an official U.S. government source. For these reasons, I doubt both the appropriateness and utility of this publication.

- The State Department's "Muslim Life in America" website (http://usinfo. state.gov/products/pubs/muslimlife/). This website is evidently designed to highlight to Muslims abroad the diversity of Muslim life in the United States. But in a well-meaning effort gone askew, this website focuses almost exclusively on very religious Muslims. It offers an image of America as the land where virtually every Muslim woman (and almost all Muslim girls) wears a veil or a headscarf. This is both factually wrong and politically counter-productive. As one scholar has noted, "Is this the message that we wish to send to the women of Afghanistan, now free to choose not to wear the burka? Is this the message we wish to send to Iranian women, battling for the right to choose their attire? Is this the message we wish to send to Turkish women, who have been at the vanguard of building a vibrant, secular democracy in an overwhelmingly Muslim state?" I think not—and I hope you agree that it is precisely the wrong message to broadcast to our allies and our enemies alike.

Mr. Secretary, I recognize that with a looming confrontation with Iraq and the ongoing effort to build international support for the war on terrorism, these matters may seem trivial. But they are not. Ideas matter. A forceful combination of advocating American interests and projecting American values was a major factor in undermining Soviet Communism from within, and the same combination can help win the long-term battle for "hearts and minds" in the global war on terrorism. In our search for allies and supporters abroad, we should never resort to sycophancy or pandering, as some of these outreach materials clearly do.

I hope, therefore, you will take urgent steps to correct these materials and ensure that America's public diplomacy remains on message, keeping faith with the interests and values that animate our great nation.

Cordially,

Tom Lantos

Abdessalam, Yassine, *Winning the Modern World for Islam*, London: Justice and Spirituality Publishing, 2000.

Abusulayman, Abdulhamid, "Chastising Women: Domestic Violence—An Islamic Response," *Islamic Horizons*, Vol. 32, No. 2, March/April 2003, p. 22.

Aggarwal, Manju, *I Am a Muslim*, New York: Franklin Watts, 1985.

Ahmed, Akbar, *Islam Today*, New York: Tauris Publications, 2001.

Ahmed, Qazi Hussain, speech at a press conference at his residence, *Indo-Asian News Service*, September 21, 2002. Online at http://www.eians.com.

Ali, Maulana Muhammad, *A Manual of Hadith*, Lahore, Pakistan: Ahamadiyya, 1992.

Ajami, Fouad, *The Arab Predicament*, Cambridge, U.K.: Cambridge University Press, 1981.

Amnesty International, "Afghanistan: Cruel, Inhuman or Degrading Treatment or Punishment," ASA 11/015/1999, November 1, 1999. Online at http://web.amnesty.org/library/index/ENGASA110151999?oper&of-ENG-AFG (as of September 3, 2003).

Ansari, Ali, *Iran, Islam and Democracy: The Politics of Managing Change*, London: Royal Institute of International Affairs, 2000.

Al-Asi, Muhammad, "The Unknown Prophet," paper presented at the International Seerah Conference, Karachi, Pakistan, June 25, 2000. Online at http://www.islamicthought.org/pp-ma-unknown.html (as of June 3, 2003).

Asian Human Rights Commission, "Pakistan," August 2, 2001. Online at http://ahrchk.net/va (circa 2002).

Al-Azmah, *Islam and Modernities*, London: Verso Publications, 1993.

Azzam, Salem, ed., *Islam and Contemporary Society*, London: Longman Publishing, 1982.

Bowcott, Owen, "Radicals Meet at North London Mosque to Mark 'Towering Day,'" *The Guardian*, September 12, 2002.

Brown, Daniel, *Rethinking Tradition in Modern Islamic Thought*, Cambridge, U.K.: Cambridge University Press, 1999.

Bush, George W., address at the Afghan embassy, Washington, D.C., September 11, 2002.

Calislar, Oral, *Islam'da Kadin ve Cinslik*, Istanbul, Turkey: Cumhuriyet Press, 1999.

Cooper, John, Ronald Nettler, and Mohamed Mahmoud, eds., *Islam and Modernity: Muslim Intellectuals Respond*, London: Tauris Publishers, 2000.

Dershowitz, Alan, and Alan Keyes, "Does Organized Religion Hold Answers to the Problems of the 21st Century?" debate, Lancaster, Pa.: Franklin and Marshall College, September 27, 2000. Online at http://www.renewamerica.us/archives/speeches/00_09_27debate.htm (as of September 8, 2003.

Doi, Abdur Rahman, "Women in Society," Zaira, Nigeria: Ahmadu Bello University, Center for Islamic Legal Studies, 2001. Online at http://www.usc.edu/dept/MSA/humanrelations/womeninislam/womeninsociety.html (as of September 8, 2003).

"Drugs and Prostitution 'Soar' in Iran," BBC News, July 6, 2000. Online at http://news.bbc.co.uk/2/hi/middle_east/822312.stm (as of June 3, 2003).

El Fadl, Khaled Abou, *Speaking in God's Name*, Oxford: One World Publishing, 2001.

"Female Fighter Pilot Sues over Required Muslim Dress," *The Washington Times*, December 4, 2001.

Fisk, Robert, "Saudis Secretly Funding Taliban," *The Independent*, September 2, 1998.

Ford, Peter, "Historic Architectural Sites Becoming Second Casualty of War in Kosovo," *Christian Science Monitor*, July 25, 2001.

Al-Ghannouchi, Rachid, "Palestine as a Global Agenda," *MSANews*, November 1999.

Gompu, Samya, "Nawal Al Saadawi Returns to the Lion's Den," *Middle East Times*, No. 22, 1995.

Green, Shaikh Abdur-Raheem, "Authenticity of the Quran," *Islamic Knowledge Bank*, Hezb-e-Islami Afghanistan, 1994. Online at http://www.hezb-e-islami.org/quran.html (as of June 3, 2003).

Gulen, Fethullah, *Key Concepts in the Practice of Sufisim*, Rochester, Mich.: Fountain Publishing, 1999.

Haddad, Yvonne Yazbeck, and Adair Lummis, *Islamic Values in the United States*, New York: Oxford University Press, 1987.

Hasan, Asma Gull, *American Muslims: The New Generation*, New York: Continuum Press, 2002.

Hashmi, Sohail, "Not What the Prophet Would Want," *The Washington Post*, June 9, 2002.

Heitmeyer, Wilhelm, interview, *Tageszeitung*, September 24, 2001.

Hizb-ut-Tahrir, *Dangerous Concepts to Attack Islam and Consolidate the Western Culture*, London: Al Khilafah Publications, 1997. Online at http://www.hizb-ut-tahrir.org/english/books/pdfs/dangerous_concepts.pdf (as of September 9, 2003).

_____, Hizb-ut-Tahrir Official Web Site, 2003. Online at http://www.hizb-ut-tahrir.org/english/ as of October 1, 2003.

Hofmann, Murad, *Islam 2000*, Beltsville, Md.: Amana Publications, 1997.

Ibn Lulu Ibn Al-Naqib, Ahmad, *The Reliance of the Traveler*, Beltsville, Md.: Amana Publications, 1997.

Iran Expert, "Hashem Aghajari: Chronology of a Crisis," November 17, 2002. Online at www.iranexpert.com/2002/chronologyofcrisis17november.htm (as of September 3, 2003).

Islam, Amatullah, "Preventing the G-B Relationship," *Nida'ul Islam Magazine*, Vol. V, No. 22, February–March 1998. Online at http://islam.org.au/articles/22/index.htm (as of June 3, 2003).

Ismaeel, Mabrook, "'Hadeeth': A Critical Evaluation with Argument and Counter-Argument," April 26, 2003. Online at http://www.submission.org/hadith/hadith2.html (as of September 3, 2003).

Islam for Today, Web site, last updated May 5, 2003. Online at http://islamfortoday.com/ (as of June 3, 2003).

Kamal Sultan, Ahmed, "Rethinking Islam, Dotting the I's and Crossing the T's," October 21, 2002. Online at http://www.islamonline.net/English/contemporary/2002/10/Article01.shtml (as of June 3, 2003).

Kaufman, Jonathan, "Islamerican," *The Wall Street Journal*, February 15, 2002, p. 1.

Kepel, Gilles, "Rechte für die Gläubigen im Gottlosen Europa: Islamistische Aktivisten umwerben junge Muslime," *Neue Zürcher Zeitung*, Dossiers, April

22, 1998. Online at http://www.nzz.ch/dossiers/islamismus/islam_kepel. html (as of June 3, 2003).

Khalid Arshed, Aneela, *The Bounty of Allah: Daily Reflections from the Quran and Islamic Tradition*, New York: Crossroad Publishing, 1999.

Kramer, Martin, "Misstating the State," *Ivory Towers on Sand,* Washington, D.C.: The Washington Institute for Near East Policy, October 2001.

Kurzman, Charles, ed., *Liberal Islam: A Sourcebook*, New York: Oxford University Press, 1998.

Lewis, Bernard, "The Roots of Muslim Rage," *The Atlantic Monthly*, September 1990.

_____, *What Went Wrong,* New York: HarperCollins Publishers, 2000.

_____, "We Must Be Clear," *The Washington Post,* September 16, 2001.

Littman, David, "Islamism Grows Stronger at the United Nations," *Middle East Forum*, September 1999.

Locke, Michelle, "Islamic Scholars Gather in California," *AP World Politics,* September 18, 2002.

Al-Mamun, Allama, *The Sayings of Muhammad*, Sacramento, Calif.: Citadel Press, 1990.

Maqsood, Ruqaiyyah, *Islam: Contemporary Books*, Chicago: McGraw-Hill, 1994a.

_____, *World Faiths: Islam*, Chicago: McGraw-Hill, 1994b.

Mardin, Serif, "Society and Islam," in John Hall, ed., *Civil Society*, Cambridge, U.K.: Polity Press, 1996.

Marquand, Robert, "The Hurricane That Swirls Over the Head Scarf," *Christian Science Monitor*, February 12, 1996.

Morris, Neil, *Islam*, New York: McGraw-Hill Children's Publishing, 2002.

Muir, Jim, "Iran's Girl Runaways," BBC News, December 14, 2000.

_____, "Iran 'Brothel' Plan Rejected," BBC News, July 28, 2002.

Our Dialogue (Islam in Perspective), Web site, online at http://ourdialogue. com/ (as of July 3, 2003).

Parwez, G. A., "Holy Quran According to Our Traditions," in G. A. Parwez, *The Status of Hadith . . . The Actual Status of Hadith*, Aboo B. Rana, tr., 2002. Online at http://www.toluislam.com/pub_online/position/hadith11.htm (as of September 8, 2003).

Al-Qaradawi, Yussef, *The Islamic Movement at Political and World Levels*, (chapter 4), *n.d.* Online at http://www.qaradawi.net (Arabic site).

Al-Rahman Al-Raheem, Bismillahi, "The System of Ruling in Islam Is Not Republican," in the From the Party Culture section, 2002. Online at http://www.hizb-ut-tahrir.org (as of June 3, 2003).

Rashid, Ahmad, *The Taliban*, New Haven, Conn.: Yale University Press, 2000.

Rauf, Abdul, "Marriage in Islam," 2002. Online at http://www.jannah.org.

Rejwan, Nissim, *Arabs Face the Modern World*, Gainesville, Fla.: University Press of Florida, 1998.

Reuters, "Pakistan Man Sentenced to Death for Blasphemy," Lahore, Pakistan, July 27, 2002.

Roy, Olivier, *The Failure of Political Islam*, Cambridge, Mass.: Harvard University Press, 1994.

Saba, Sadeq, "Rape and Murder on Rise in Tehran," BBC News, October 17, 2000.

Sachedina, Abdulaziz, *The Islamic Roots of Democratic Pluralism*, New York: Oxford University Press, 2001.

Schwartz, Stephen, "The Arab Betrayal of Balkan Islam," *Middle East Quarterly*, Spring 2002.

Schwarzer, Alice, ed., *Die Gotteskrieger und die falsche Toleranz [On Holy Warriors and Misplaced Tolerance]*, Cologne, Germany: Kiepenheuer & Witsch, 2002.

Shahrur, Muhammad, "Proposal for an Islamic Covenant," Damascus 2000, 2000. Online at http://www.islam21.net/pages/charter/may-1.htm (as of September 9, 2003).

Smith, Jane, *Islam in America*, New York: Columbia University Press, 1999.

Tibi, Bassam, *The Crisis of Modern Islam*, Salt Lake City, Utah: University of Utah Press, 1988.

_____, "Die Deutsche Verordnete Fremdenliebe," in Schwarzer (2002), pp. 105–120.

Toward Tomorrow (Web site on Fethullah Gulen), last updated August 28, 2003. Online at http://www.mfgulen.com (as of September 8, 2003).

UNDP—*see* United Nations Development Programme.

United Nations Development Programme, *Arab Human Development Report 2002*, New York: United Nations, 2002.

U.S. Department of State, *Muslim Life in America,* http://usinfo.state.gov/products/pubs/muslimlife/ (as of September 9, 2003).

Wadud, Amina, *Quran and Woman: Rereading the Sacred Text from a Woman's Perspective,* New York: Oxford University Press, 1999.

Warraq, Ibn, *Why I Am Not a Muslim,* New York: Prometheus, 1995.

Wax, Emily, "The Fabric of Their Faith," *The Washington Post,* May 19, 2002.

Wiseman, Paul, "Words Can Bring Death Sentence in Pakistan," *USA Today,* March 25, 2002.

Made in the USA